Practical English Language Teaching: Reading

BY

NEIL J. ANDERSON

SERIES EDITOR: DAVID NUNAN

Practical English Language Teaching: Reading

Published by McGraw-Hill ESL/ELT, a business unit of The McGraw-Hill Companies, Inc. 1221 Avenue of the Americas, New York, NY 10020. Copyright © 2008 by The McGraw-Hill Companies, Inc. All rights reserved. No part of this publication may be reproduced or distributed in any form or by any means, or stored in a database or retrieval system, without the prior written consent of The McGraw-Hill Companies, Inc., including, but not limited to, in any network or other electronic storage or transmission, or broadcast for distance learning.

 This book is printed on recycled, acid-free paper containing 10% post-consumer waste.

ISBN 13: 978-0-07-338459-7
ISBN 10: 0-07-338459-3

1 2 3 4 5 6 7 8 9 10 DOC 12 11 10 09 08

Project Manager: Linda O'Roke
Cover designer: Martini Graphic Services, Inc.
Interior designer: Acento Visual

Acknowledgements

I would like to thank the following individuals who reviewed the *Practical English Language Teaching* and *Practical English Language Teaching: Reading* manuscripts at various stages of development, and whose commentary was instrumental in shaping these professional reference volumes:

Kathleen M. Bailey, Monterey Institute of International Studies, Monterey, California, USA

Ronald Carter, Centre for English Language Education, Department of English Studies, University of Nottingham, UK

Andy Curtis, Chinese University of Hong Kong, PRC

Nicholas Dimmitt, Asian Institute of Technology, Pathumthani, Thailand

Fernando Fleurquin, ALIANZA, Montevideo, Uruguay

Donald Freeman, School for International Training, Brattleboro, Vermont, USA

Donald Occhuizzo, World Learning/School for International Training; formerly Alumni, Sao Paulo, Brazil

Betsy Parrish, Hamline University, St. Paul, Minnesota, USA

Michael Rost, Author/Researcher, San Francisco, California, USA

Kathy Z. Weed

In addition, I want to thank **David Nunan**, the series editor, for continuing to encourage me to complete this project. He has a clear vision of the *Practical English Language Teaching* series and how it can assist teachers in improving their work in the classroom.

My critical buddy for this project was **Kathleen M. Bailey**. Kathi has been a mentor for me in various roles. This is the first time we have worked closely on a book. I would gladly enter into another such project if I could work with her. Kathi has a keen sense of what will (and what will not) make sense to new and veteran teachers.

The members of the editorial team at McGraw-Hill ESL/ELT–**Erik Gundersen** and **Linda O'Roke** are exceptional people to work with. Linda knows how to push a writer to improve the quality of the product.

Thank you all for your encouragement and input on this contribution to the *Practical English Language Teaching* series!

This book is dedicated to my newest granddaughter, **Riley Dawnielle Anderson**, who was born a few weeks before completion of this book. Papa Neil looks forward to reading many great stories with you throughout your life.

Table of Contents

Foreword

Vision and purpose

The *Practical English Language Teaching* series is designed for practicing teachers or teachers in preparation who may or may not have formal training in second and foreign language teaching methodology. The core volume in this series, *Practical English Language Teaching*, provides an overall introduction to key aspects of language teaching methodology in an accessible yet not trivial way. The purpose of this book is to explore the teaching of reading in greater depth than was possible in the core volume, while at the same time remaining both comprehensive and accessible.

Features

- A clear orientation to the teaching of reading including important definitions, an introduction to the processes behind reading, and a look at the overall approach to teaching reading in the classroom.

- A detailed treatment of the teaching of reading at the beginner, intermediate, and advanced levels providing practical techniques for teaching and assessing reading at each of these levels.

- Reflection questions inviting readers to think about critical issues in language teaching and Action tasks requiring readers to apply the ideas, principles and techniques to the teaching of reading in their own situation.

- A great deal of practical illustration from a wide range of textbooks as well as discussion of how to apply the textbooks in the classroom.

- A "key issues" chapter that looks at reading beyond the classroom and provides suggestions for dealing with the use of technology and catering to different learning styles and strategies. This chapter also features tips from leading researchers and teachers of reading.

- Suggestions for books, articles and websites offering resources for additional up-to-date information.

- Expansive glossary offers short and straightforward definitions of core language teaching terms.

Audience

As with the overview volume, this book is designed for both experienced and novice teachers. It should also be of value to those who are about to join the profession. It will update the experienced teacher on current theoretical and practical approaches to teaching reading. The novice teacher will find step-by-step guidance on the practice of teaching reading.

Overview

Chapter 1

The first chapter provides an orientation to reading in a second or foreign language. The chapter also introduces key principles for teaching and assessing reading.

Chapters 2–4

Chapters 2–4 introduce you to the teaching of reading to beginning, intermediate, and advanced students respectively. Each chapter follows the format below.

Chapter 5

The final chapter starts off with top-five lists of priorities for reading teachers from top researchers and teachers in the field. The chapter also focuses on the importance of bottom-up reading skills, the need for silent and oral reading fluency, more extensive reading in the classroom, and the continuation of professional development for reading teachers.

Chapter structure for Chapters 2–4

Goals: Summarizes what you should know and be able to do after having read the chapter and completed the Reflection and Action boxes.

Introduction: Gives an overview of the chapter.

Syllabus design issues: Outlines the approaches to reading that are relevant at different levels.

Principles for teaching reading: Appropriate principles for teaching reading at different levels are introduced, discussed, and illustrated.

Tasks and materials: Describes and illustrates techniques and exercises for teaching reading at each level.

Reading inside and outside of the classroom: Introduces issues such as lesson planning that affect what we do in the classroom.

Techniques for assessment: Introduces practical techniques for assessing learners in the classroom.

Conclusion: Reviews the goals of the chapter and how they were discussed within the chapter.

Further Readings: Lists articles or books to enhance your knowledge of teaching reading.

Helpful Websites: Provides ideas for web resources for teaching reading.

Chapter **One**

What is reading?

At the end of this chapter, you should be able to:

 provide your own definition of reading.

 identify reasons why establishing a culture of reading both inside and outside of the classroom is important.

 describe the differences among bottom-up, top-down, and interactive reading.

 explain intensive and extensive reading and how each can be integrated into a reading curriculum.

 identify reading strategies that language learners can use to improve their reading.

 describe why the assessment of reading is important to the successful teaching of reading.

1. Introduction

The purpose of this book is to provide you with an opportunity to think about techniques and strategies to improve the teaching of reading to students of **English as a Second Language (ESL)** or **English as a Foreign Language (EFL)**. Each chapter of the book will provide helpful suggestions that you can use in the classroom to engage learners in meaningful ways to improve their reading.

This chapter will focus on the concept of reading. We will first answer the question, *What is reading?* The importance of establishing a culture of reading will then be discussed. We will explore the concepts of bottom-up, top-down, and interactive reading. Next, we will explore intensive and extensive reading and identify how both can be integrated into a reading curriculum. This discussion will be followed by identifying the importance of reading strategies that language learners can use to improve their reading. Finally, we will discuss how to balance the teaching and assessment of reading.

Keep in mind that the overall goal of this book is to be a guide and a resource to you as a teacher to make the teaching of reading more accessible. Whether you are teaching reading as a separate skill, teaching reading as part of an integrated skills approach, or teaching a **content area** in which students engage in reading, this book will give you ideas for how to help the students you work with to be better readers. You will learn very specific things that you can do to be more confident about teaching reading.

2. What is reading?

Write a short definition of reading on the lines below. Underline key words in your definition that you feel are essential to understanding what reading is.

_____

_____

_____

Share your definition with a classmate or colleague.

_____

Reading can be defined simply as making meaning from print. Four key elements combine in the process of making meaning from print: the reader, the text, reading strategies, and fluency. Reading is a process of readers combining information from a text and their own background knowledge to build meaning. Meaning does not rest in the reader nor does it rest in the text. The reader's background knowledge integrates with the text to create the meaning. The goal of reading is comprehension. **Fluent reading** is defined as the ability to read at an appropriate rate with adequate comprehension. **Strategic reading** is defined as the ability of the reader to use a wide variety of reading strategies to accomplish a purpose for reading. Good strategic readers know what to do when they encounter difficulties. The text, the reader, strategies, and fluency together define the act of reading. See Figure 1 for a visual representation of the definition of reading.

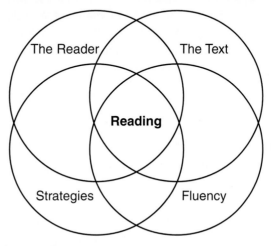

Figure 1: The definition of reading

Notice that the intersection of all four circles represents reading. This is the point where meaningful reading happens. Grabe (1991) points out the complexity of even defining reading by stating that "a description of reading has to account for the notions that fluent reading is rapid, purposeful, interactive, comprehending, flexible, and gradually developing" (p. 378).

Meaning is at the core of what reading is. If no meaning is communicated then something other than reading is happening. There is an expectation that when we read, we will do something with what we have read. For example, we will place a phone call to the correct telephone number because we have found the number in the telephone book. Or we will talk to a family member or a friend about something that we have read. We will write a report based on information we have collected through reading. We will simply read to receive pleasure. No matter the outcome, we should remember that there is a reason why we are reading.

Teaching reading usually has at least two aspects. In one aspect, it can refer to teaching children who are learning to read in their first language for the very first time. (This book will not focus on literacy instruction. Please refer to Chapter 4 of *Practical English Language Teaching: Young Learners* for information on teaching reading to young native and non-native learners of

English (Linse, 2005).) A second aspect of teaching reading refers to teaching learners who already have reading skills in their first language. Like learning how to ride a bicycle, you only have to learn to read once. Once you have learned how to read in one language, you do not learn how to read again in a second or foreign language. Rather you need to learn how to transfer skills that you have already learned in your first language to new reading contexts in a new language.

Action

Compare the definition of reading that you wrote on page 2 with the definition given in this section. What elements of your definition are contained in the definition given? What elements of your definition are *not* contained in the definition given? What changes (if any) would you make in your definition now? Rewrite your definition below.

_____

_____

_____

Share your new definition with a classmate or colleague.

_____

Establishing a culture of reading

As I entered my ESL reading class one day, my Mexican students wanted to share a joke that they had made up. They asked, "When you're on a beach in Mexico (or any place in the world), how do you know who the Americans are?" I suggested answers like the color of the skin or the use of English. The response was "No, no, teacher! The Americans are reading books and the Mexicans are not." They found it humorous to make fun of their own culture.

In many places of the world, reading is not an integral part of people's lives. As teachers, one of our goals should be to excite our students so that they will want to read. Our students should see from our enthusiasm that gaining information and knowledge from reading is an important part of our lives.

I believe that there are three reasons why we should consider the importance of establishing a culture of reading. First, much of the information available in the world comes in the format of print. Most of the printed materials in the world come in English. In order to help students access more of the information available in English, the teacher must establish a culture of reading.

Next, reading strengthens other areas of learning. For the second language learners we work with, this means that reading can strengthen the learning of writing, listening, and speaking. If you read well, you then have something to talk and write about. You can listen to others talk about the subject as well. Also, reading is a way to learn new information as you read content area material. As you learn new things through reading, you improve your overall learning.

Finally, establishing a culture of reading can lead to increased critical thinking skills. If you talk to people who read a lot, they often read many different opinions on a topic. They are able to sift through arguments and arrive at a position because they have critically developed their ideas.

Reflection

Do you believe that you currently teach or will be teaching in a program that has a well-established culture of reading? Why or why not? What could you do as a teacher of reading to help build or strengthen a culture of reading where you teach?

Share your answers with a classmate or colleague.

Bottom-up, top-down, and interactive reading

Bottom-up, top-down, and interactive reading are names of different theoretical models that researchers use to describe how people process print. We will review each of these models and gain an understanding of why an interactive process is the best representation of how people read.

Bottom-up models consist of lower-level reading processes. Students start with the fundamental basics of letter and sound recognition, which in turn allows them to move up to morpheme recognition followed by word recognition, building up to the identification of grammatical structures, sentences, and longer texts. Understanding letters, letter clusters, words, phrases, sentences, longer text, and finally meaning is the order in achieving comprehension. With the bottom-up model, students start from the bottom (letters and sounds) to get to the top (comprehension).

A **phonics approach** to teaching reading supports a bottom-up model. Phonics focuses on learning individual letters and sounds rather than learning a word as a whole unit. This approach is used in many reading series. Many teachers and researchers suggest that for readers to be successful, they must be able to break a word down into its smallest parts, the individual sounds. When readers come to an unknown word, they can sound out the word because of the knowledge of the individual units that make up the word. The blending together of the various sounds allows readers to then move toward comprehension. Teachers must remember that phonics is a method, *not* the goal for teaching reading. Cummins (2003) emphasizes that "the purpose of phonics instruction should be to facilitate access to and comprehension of meaningful print" (p. 18). This means that our goal is not to teach phonics but to use phonics as a method to develop readers' bottom-up skills, leading to comprehension of the material being read.

One element of a bottom-up approach to reading is that the pedagogy recommends a graded-reader approach. All reading material is carefully reviewed so that students are not exposed to vocabulary that contains sounds that they have not yet been introduced to.

Figure 2 is a graphic representation of a bottom-up approach to reading. The reader begins with the smallest elements and builds up to comprehension of what is being read.

Comprehension

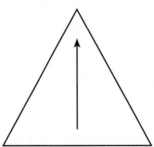

Reading begins with individual letters and sounds

Figure 2: A bottom-up approach to reading

Top-down reading, on the other hand, begins with the idea that comprehension resides in the reader. The reader uses background knowledge, makes predictions, and searches the text to confirm or reject the predictions that are made. Grabe and Stoller (2002) point out that in a top-down model of reading, comprehension is directed by the reader's goals and expectations. A reading passage can thus be understood even if not all of the individual words are understood. Within a top-down approach to reading, the teacher focuses on meaning-generating activities rather than on mastery of the bottom-up skills of letter, sound, and word recognition.

Goodman (1976), one of the original advocates of top-down models of reading, criticizes bottom-up models because the readers become "word callers," people who can read the words on the page but do not understand what they have read. Goodman believes that teachers make learning to read difficult "by breaking whole (natural) language into bite-sized, abstract little pieces" (p. 7). I agree somewhat with him. For example, I can read Spanish and pronounce all of the words that I'm reading correctly, and yet depending on what I am reading, I may have no comprehension of what I have read.

A meaning-based approach or a whole-language approach to reading is supportive of top-down models of reading. Four key features highlight a meaning-based or whole-language approach to teaching reading. First, it is a literature-based approach. Books are used which contain authentic language. Readers are exposed to a wide range of vocabulary. Next, whole language is student-centered with the focus on individual readers choosing what they want to read. Third, reading is integrated with writing. Classes work on both skills simultaneously. Finally, emphasis is on constructing meaning. The focus is on meaning and keeping the language whole, as opposed to breaking it down into smaller units. Whole language is an approach, *not* the goal. The goal is reading comprehension. One possible way to help students understand their reading is to use a whole-language approach to teaching.

Figure 3 is a graphic representation of a top-down approach to reading. The reader begins with the largest elements and works down towards smaller elements to build comprehension of what is being read.

Reading begins with reader background knowledge

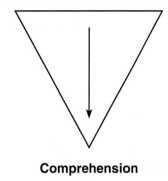

Comprehension

Figure 3: A top-down approach to reading

The approach that is accepted as the most comprehensive description of the reading process is an **interactive approach**. This third type combines elements of both bottom-up and top-down approaches. The best readers in any language are those who combine elements of both. For example, most readers begin reading by using top-down reading strategies until there is a problem, and then they shift to bottom-up strategies. Have you ever read something quickly and suddenly come to several new words? You are required to slow down your reading to decode the new words. When you do this, you are using bottom-up strategies to understand the words.

Figure 4 is a graphic representation of an interactive approach to reading. The reader combines elements of both bottom-up and top-down models of reading to reach comprehension.

Reader background knowledge

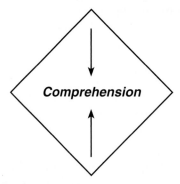

Comprehension

Knowledge of individual letters and sounds

Figure 4: An interactive approach to reading.

Reflection

If you have studied a second language, can you identify the approach to the teaching of reading that was used when you learned to read in that language? If you currently teach a class, can you identify the approach to the teaching of reading that is used in your program? Is the approach a bottom-up one? Top-down? Or interactive? What is it about your program that leads you to your decision? What could you do to strengthen an interactive approach to teaching reading? If you are not yet teaching, think of a program you are familiar with. Is the approach to reading a bottom-up, top-down, or interactive approach?

Share your answers with a classmate or colleague.

Intensive and extensive reading

Reading is best developed through reading and not through talking about reading. Two basic approaches are used for teaching reading: **intensive reading** and **extensive reading**. The differences between intensive and extensive reading are important for teachers to understand. Intensive reading is the teaching of reading skills, vocabulary, and phonological instruction, typically through short reading passages followed by reading comprehension exercises. Extensive reading is reading of longer passages with a focus on enjoyment and/or learning new information while reading. There is typically no accountability required during extensive reading.

A bottom-up approach to reading would be considered part of intensive reading. Teachers would focus classroom time on learning individual letters and sounds and provide many practice opportunities for the learners. Extensive reading plays a key role in top-down approaches to reading. Extensive reading means reading many books (or longer segments of text) without focusing on classroom exercises that may test comprehension skills.

An interactive approach to reading would include aspects of both intensive and extensive reading. As teachers, we need to provide learners with shorter passages to explicitly teach specific reading skills. We also need to encourage learners to read longer texts without an emphasis on testing their skills. Extensive reading provides opportunities to practice skills introduced during intensive reading instruction, and it can lead to increased enjoyment of reading.

Teachers should be aware that a single classroom textbook will not meet the needs for both intensive and extensive instruction. Materials will need to be selected that engage the learners in both types of reading.

Figure 5 outlines a way that we can view the relationships between intensive and extensive reading.

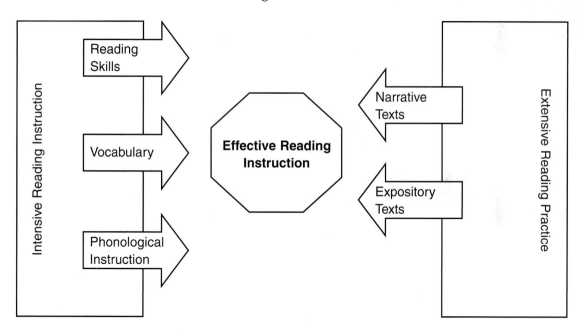

Figure 5: The integration of intensive and extensive reading

Note that during intensive reading instruction, teachers can explicity teach reading skills and vocabulary and provide phonological instruction so that learners have the tools to read effectively. Then learners read extensively in order to practice their developing reading skills with longer texts. By combining both intensive and extensive reading in the same program, more effective reading instruction can occur.

Write three advantages to establishing a reading curriculum that includes both intensive and extensive reading opportunities for the learners.

1. _____

2. _____

3. _____

Share your list with a classmate or colleague.

Reflection

With a classmate or colleague, discuss any disadvantages or challenges you see in establishing a reading program that includes both intensive and extensive reading opportunities for learners.

Reading strategies

Perhaps one aspect of teaching reading that teachers might know about, but often do not know how to do, is the explicit teaching of **reading strategies**. Perceptive second-language readers are those who are aware of and use appropriate reading strategies for learning in a second language. The purpose of teaching reading strategies is to improve comprehension while reading. Strategies are the *conscious* actions that readers take to improve their **reading skills**. Strategies may be mental but observable, such as observing someone taking notes while reading to recall information better, or strategies may be mental and unobservable, such as thinking about what one already knows on a topic before reading a passage. Because strategies are conscious, there is active involvement of the reader in their selection and use.

Strategies are not isolated actions, but rather a process of orchestrating more than one action to accomplish an **L2**–second language–task. It may be helpful to view strategy use as an orchestra. An instrument sounds good alone, but when combined with other instruments, a much stronger, more glorious sound results. Although we can identify individual strategies, rarely will one strategy be used in isolation. Strategies are related to each other and must be viewed as a part of a process, not as a single action. Also, it is important to understand that we do not categorize strategies as good or bad, but rather it is the implementation and use of the strategies which are considered good or bad.

Perhaps you are familiar with various learning strategy inventories that are available such as Oxford's (1990) *Strategy Inventory for Language Learning* (SILL). The SILL is perhaps the most widely used strategy inventory for language learning. Teachers in many countries of the world use this inventory as a tool in raising the awareness of language learning strategies. The SILL contains 50 items and provides learners with a profile of strategy use in six areas: memory strategies, cognitive strategies, compensation strategies, metacognitive strategies, affective strategies, and social strategies. Cohen, Oxford, and Chi (2001) have developed the *Language Strategy Use Survey.* This survey includes revised items from the SILL as well as strategies identified and described in Cohen's (1990) *Language Learning: Insights for Learners, Teachers, and Researchers,* and those included in Paige, Cohen, Kappler, Chi, and Lassegard, (2002) *Maximizing Study Abroad.* Like the SILL, the *Language Strategy Use Survey* can serve as a tool to raise awareness of strategy use. The major difference between the SILL and the survey is that the *Language Strategy Use Survey* focuses on the use of strategies in specific language skills. The survey asks learners to rate their strategy use in six specific sections: listening strategies, vocabulary strategies, speaking strategies, reading strategies, writing strategies, and translation strategies.

An additional inventory that shows great promise is a more recent instrument developed by Mokhtari and reported in Mokhtari and Sheorey (2002) and Sheorey and Mokhtari (2001). The *Survey of Reading Strategies* (SORS) focuses on **metacognitive strategy** use within the context of reading. The SORS measures three categories of reading strategies: global reading strategies (e.g., having a purpose for reading, using context to guess unfamiliar vocabulary, confirming or rejecting your predictions), problem-solving strategies (e.g., adjusting reading rate, focusing when concentration is lost), and support strategies (e.g., taking notes while reading, highlighting important ideas in the text). Since it has just recently been completed, more studies need to be conducted using this instrument in order to better understand the use of specific strategies in ESL and EFL contexts.

I use the SORS as a tool to introduce learners to the concept of reading strategies. The inventory helps make readers more aware of the kinds of strategies that good readers use. By introducing strategies at the beginning of the semester, I'm then able to integrate the explicit teaching of strategies throughout the rest of the semester. In Chapters 2–5, we will discuss how to effectively introduce the teaching of strategies to help learners be effective readers.

The *Survey of Reading Strategies* (SORS) is in Appendix 1 (pages 155–158). Please respond to the questions to get a profile of your reading strategies. Then complete the questions below.

1. What do you learn about yourself as a strategic reader from your SORS profile?

_____

_____

_____

2. How could you use the SORS with second-language readers?

_____

_____

_____

Share your responses with a classmate or colleague.

Assessing reading

The assessment of reading is vital in order to help learners see the progress that they are making. Assessing growth and development in reading skills from both a formal and an informal perspective requires time and training. Formal assessments are often **quantitative** in nature. For example, a formal assessment of reading would be a reading comprehension test in which the students are graded on the percentage of correct answers. Many intensive reading books available commercially have a reading passage followed by comprehension questions. This type of feedback to the learner is useful in giving them information about how well they are reading.

Qualitative assessments include assessments that do not result in a numerical score. Reading interest surveys, reading strategy surveys (such as the SORS referred to earlier in this chapter), interviews, journal responses, and portfolios are examples of qualitative assessments. Qualitative assessment activities should also be included in the reading classroom. In each of the chapters that follow, we will identify appropriate ways to assess reading both qualitatively and quantitatively.

Action

Respond to the following multiple-choice questions about issues discussed in this chapter. This is an example of a formal, quantitative assessment of your understanding of key issues discussed in this chapter.

1. What are the four key elements needed to make meaning from print?
   A. The reader, content, culture, and fluency
   B. The text, top-down processes, bottom-up processes, and interactive processes
   C. Strategies, fluency, the text, and the reader
   D. Fluency, content, interactive processes, and intensive reading

2. Which of the following is *not* one of the reasons given in this chapter for establishing a culture of reading?
   A. Reading helps students enjoy life.
   B. To access printed material
   C. Reading strengthens other areas of learning.
   D. To increase critical thinking skills

3. Which graphic best represents an interactive model for reading?

   A.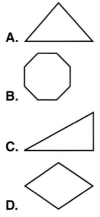

   B.

   C.

   D.

4. Intensive reading focuses on the following aspects of reading:
   A. Effective reading instruction with many opportunities to read
   B. Reading skills, vocabulary, and phonological instruction
   C. Narrative and expository texts to expose readers to variety
   D. All of the above

5. What is the purpose of teaching reading strategies?
   A. To improve reading comprehension
   B. To help readers be more perceptive
   C. To help readers be conscious of their learning
   D. To gather research data to improve teaching

Turn to page 17 at the end of this chapter to find the correct answers to this quiz and determine your score.

Respond to the following reading journal prompts. This is an example of an informal, qualitative assessment of your understanding of key issues discussed in this chapter.

1. Identify five things that you have learned in this chapter.

_____

_____

_____

_____

_____

_____

2. How will the information in this chapter help you to be a better second-language teacher?

_____

_____

_____

_____

_____

_____

3. How can you use the *Further Readings* and the *Helpful Websites* listed below to help you learn more about improving your teaching skills?

_____

_____

_____

_____

_____

_____

Share your answers with a classmate or colleague.

3. Conclusion

The goal of this chapter has been to focus on the concept of reading and to introduce a number of factors to consider when we are deciding how it can be taught. We first addressed the question, *What is reading?* We identified that the text, the reader, strategies, and fluency combine to define the act of reading. The importance of establishing a culture of reading was also discussed. We then explored the concepts of bottom-up, top-down, and interactive reading. Next, we examined intensive and extensive reading and identified how both can be integrated into a reading curriculum. We also discussed how reading strategies play a central role to successful reading. Finally, we identified the importance of balancing both the teaching and assessment of reading. Each of these ideas will be consider in more depth in the next three chapters.

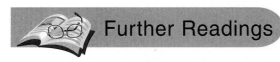 **Further Readings**

Volumes of material have been written about how to teach second-language reading. Publications that I have found particularly useful include:

Anderson, N.J. 1999. *Exploring Second Language Reading: Issues and strategies.* Boston, MA: Heinle & Heinle.

In this book, I outline an approach to reading based around the acronym ACTIVE: activate prior knowledge, cultivate vocabulary, teach for comprehension, increase reading rate, verify strategies, and evaluate progress. Helpful suggestions are provided for teachers to implement an active approach to reading instruction.

Bamford, J. and R. Day. 2004. *Extensive Reading Activities for Teaching Language.* New York, NY: Cambridge University Press.

This book provides over 100 practical activities that teachers can use in the classroom to encourage extensive reading. The book is divided into 13 sections: (1) getting started, (2) introducing reading material, (3) motivating and supporting reading, (4) monitoring reading, (5) evaluating reading, (6) oral reading reports, (7) drama and role plays, (8) having fun, (9) written reading reports, (10) writing creatively, (11) developing awareness in reading, (12) increasing reading rate, and (13) developing and consolidating vocabulary. The book ends with a useful section on the 12 most frequently asked questions about extensive reading.

Brown, J. D. 2005. *Testing in language programs: A comprehensive guide to English language assessment. (New edition).* New York, NY: McGraw-Hill.

This book approaches essential testing principles in a way that can help all teachers write strong language assessments. The 11 chapters cover: types and uses of tests; adopting, adapting, and developing language tests; developing good-quality language test items; item analysis in language testing; describing language test results; interpreting language test scores; correlation in language testing; language test reliability; language test dependability; language test validity; and language testing in reality.

Grabe, W. and F. Stoller. 2002. *Teaching and Researching Reading.* New York, NY: Pearson Education.

Grabe and Stoller provide useful information for both teachers and researchers interested in second-language reading. The 10 chapters are divided into four sections: understanding L2 reading, exploring research in reading, researching reading in the classroom, and resources.

Hudson, T. 2007. *Teaching second language reading.* New York, NY: Oxford University Press.

This new book by Hudson covers several issues of importance to teachers of reading. The book includes chapters on theories and models of first language reading processes, second and foreign language reading issues, reading skills, strategies and metacognitive skills, content schema and background knowledge, formal schema and second language reading, genre and contrastive rhetoric, vocabulary in second language reading, reading and writing relationships, and teaching issues.

Koda, K. 2005. *Insights into Second Language Reading.* New York, NY: Cambridge University Press.

This book is theoretically based, examining models for both first- and second-language reading. Koda's work provides one of the best written books to examine the theories of reading. In particular she identifies new directions for research into the complex processes of second-language reading. Readers who are interested in doing research related to second-language reading should read this book.

Helpful Websites

Extensive Reading (www.extensivereading.net/)

This is a very useful site to learn more about extensive reading. The site provides links to many articles that are accessible online about different aspects of extensive reading.

Language Strategy Use Survey (www.carla.umn.edu/about/profiles/CohenPapers/Lg_Strat_Srvy.pdf)

Cohen, Oxford, and Chi's (2001) *Language Strategy Use Survey* is available online. The survey includes revised items from Oxford's *Strategy Inventory for Language Learning* as well as strategies identified and described in Cohen's (1990) *Language Learning: Insights for Learners, Teachers, and Researchers*, and those included in Paige, Cohen, Kappler, Chi, and Lassegard, *Maximizing Study Abroad*.

References

Cohen, A.D. 1990. *Language Learning: Insights for Learners, Teachers, and Researchers.* New York, NY: Newbury House Publishers.

Cohen, A.D., R.L. Oxford, and J.C. Chi. 2001. *Language Strategy Use Survey.* Minneapolis, MN: Center for Advanced Research on Language Acquisition, University of Minnesota.

Cummins, J. 2003. Reading and the Bilingual Student: Fact and friction. In G.G. Garcia (Ed.) *English Learners: Reaching the highest level of English literacy* (pp. 2–33). Newark, DE: International Reading Association.

Goodman, K. 1976. Reading: A psycholinguistic guessing game. In H. Singer and R.B. Ruddell (Eds.) *Theoretical Models and Processes of Reading,* 2nd ed. (pp. 497–508). Newark, DE: International Reading Association.

Grabe, W. 1991. Current Developments in Second Language Reading Research. *TESOL Quarterly, 25,* 375–406.

Linse, C.T. 2005. *Practical English Language Teaching: Young Learners.* New York. NY: McGraw Hill.

Mokhtari, K., and R. Sheorey. 2002. Measuring ESL Students' Awareness of Reading Strategies. *Journal of Developmental Education, 25*(3), 2–10.

Oxford, R.L. 1990. *Language Learning Strategies: What every teacher should know.* New York, NY: Newbury House Publishers.

Paige, R.M., A.D. Cohen, B. Kappler, J.C. Chi and J.P. Lassegard. 2002. *Maximizing Study Abroad: A student's guide to strategies for language and culture learning and use.* Minneapolis, MN: Center for Advanced Research on Language Acquisition.

Sheorey, R. and K. Mokhtari. 2001. Differences in the Metacognitive Awareness of Reading Strategies among Native and Non-native Readers. *System, 29,* 431–449.

Answers to the multiple-choice quiz from page 13.

1. C	**2.** A	**3.** D	**4.** B	**5.** A

Correct answers	Percentage
5	100%
4	80%
3	60%
2	40%
1	20%
0	0%

Chapter **Two**

Reading for beginning level learners

At the end of this chapter, you should be able to:

Goals

✔ **describe** how reading is typically taught to learners at beginning levels of language proficiency.

✔ **explain** the differences between teaching reading and testing reading comprehension.

✔ **identify** reading strategies appropriate for beginning level readers.

✔ **recognize** principles of teaching beginning level readers.

✔ **explain** five different purposes for assessment: placement tests, diagnostic tests, progress tests, achievement tests, and learner self-assessment.

1. Introduction

In the *Practical English Language Teaching* series, the level of language proficiency (beginning, intermediate, and advanced) is used as the organizing framework. In this volume, we will refer to descriptors developed within the Common European Framework (CEF) for teaching reading (Council of Europe, 2001). In terms of describing the teaching of reading, the CEF has three levels: basic user (beginning), independent user (intermediate), and proficient user (advanced). Each of these three levels is further subdivided into two levels. The label *Basic user* is subdivided into levels A1, referred to as the *Breakthrough* level and A2, referred to as the *Waystage* level. In this chapter, we will address the issues dealing with this first stage of English language proficiency and ways to teach reading.

In this book, we do not address the issues of teaching initial literacy skills to second language (L2) readers. As it is addressed here, beginning level readers are readers that are literate in their first language but are at the beginning stages of learning to read in English. *Beginning* refers to a level of language proficiency and not a beginning reader. In second language learning contexts, we also often use the term **false beginners** to refer to learners who are not beginning initial reading instruction. They have received minimal instruction in English and have some reading ability but are still at a beginning level of English language proficiency. You will see from the CEF descriptors below that we will refer primarily to false beginners in this chapter.

It is very important to understand that the way a learner at the beginning level of language proficiency is defined in one language program may be different from the way that you define it. In Chapter 3, we will address how to teach reading to independent users, and in Chapter 4, we will look at ways to improve teaching to proficient users.

In Section 2 of this chapter, we will look at **syllabus** design issues in teaching reading. In Section 3, we will examine principles that can guide the teaching of reading to beginners. This will be followed in Section 4 with an examination of appropriate tasks and materials for beginning level learners. Section 5 will allow us to address issues of teaching reading inside and outside of the classroom. The role of assessment with readers who are at the beginning level of language proficiency is addressed in Section 6.

Reflection

Do you know someone who is a beginning level reader? What characteristics make this person a beginner?

Share your ideas with a classmate or colleague.

How can we best define a beginning level reader? The Common European Framework (CEF) descriptors indicate that a *Breakthrough user* (beginning level) of English can:

- understand very short, simple texts a single phrase at a time, picking up familiar names, words, and basic phrases and rereading as required.
- understand short, simple messages on postcards.
- recognize familiar names, words, and very basic phrases on simple notices in the most common everyday situations.
- get an idea of the content of simpler informational material and short simple descriptions, especially if there is visual support.
- follow short, simple written directions (e.g., go from X to Y).

A *Waystage user* (also a beginning level) of English can:

- read very short, simple texts.
- find specific, predictable information in simple everyday material such as advertisements, prospectuses, menus, and timetables on familiar topics.
- understand short, simple personal letters.
- understand short, simple texts containing the highest frequency vocabulary, including a portion of shared international vocabulary items.
- locate specific information in lists and isolate the information required (e.g., Yellow pages to find a service provider).
- understand everyday signs and notices in public places, such as streets, restaurants, and railway stations, and in work places such as instructions, directions, and warnings.

The information above helps us understand that with beginning level readers our primary purpose will be to help them be able to move beyond reading isolated words and phrases to reading connected text.

Action

Write three things that you think are important to teach to a beginning level reader.

1. _____

2. _____

3. _____

Find someone you know who is a beginning level reader. Ask them to identify the three things they want most to be taught. Write them here.

1. _____

2. _____

3. _____

Compare the two lists. How are your ideas of what should be taught to a beginning level learner similar to and different from what the beginning level learner told you?

_____

_____

_____

_____

_____

Share your answers with a classmate or colleague.

_____

2. Syllabus design issues

In Chapter 1, I used the two terms **English as a Second Language (ESL)** and **English as a Foreign Language (EFL)**. ESL is the study of English in an environment where English is the language of communication outside of the classroom (e.g., learning English in England or New Zealand) while EFL is the study of English in an environment where English is *not* the language of communication outside of the classroom (e.g., learning English in Brazil or Korea).

Notice these key words in the definition: *the language of communication.* Communication is typically identified as *oral communication.* However, for the context of this book, *communication* refers to written communication–communication between a reader and a writer. As teachers of reading, our role is to identify appropriate pieces of communication that will allow our beginning learners to process the information successfully.

In my research (Anderson, 2004), I have noted that when addressing the language skill of reading, it may no longer be useful to use the ESL/EFL dichotomy. As I stated:

> In terms of L2 reading, the traditional dichotomy between ESL and EFL learners may not be as important today as it has been in previous years. L2 readers around the world have increased opportunities for exposure to English. The Internet and availability of good pedagogical materials are reaching learners in many parts of the world today. L2 teachers are better prepared to teach reading than 30 years ago. This exposure to English by capable, qualified teachers provides increased

opportunities for input in English and thus decreases the differences between readers in the traditional ESL/EFL dichotomy (page 12).

Reflection

What is your reaction to the statement above? Do you agree that the distinction between ESL and EFL is fading in terms of teaching reading? Why do you agree or disagree?

Share your answer with a classmate or colleague.

The important point from my statement quoted above is that as teachers of reading, we have increased access to input and appropriate communication to share with our learners. We should approach the development of a reading syllabus with the intention of providing our readers with appropriate input. Regardless of where one lives in the world, input for reading is more easily accessible today than at any other point in the history of language teaching and learning. We should look for opportunities to capitalize on this benefit.

The organizational framework most frequently used in textbooks designed to teach reading is thematic topics. Example 1 below is the table of contents from two recently published reading textbooks. Notice the thematic topics that have been selected for each book.

Example 1

Read and Reflect 1	*Themes for Today,* 2nd ed.
Unit 1: Reaching Out	**Unit 1:** Home and Family
Unit 2: A Need for Privacy	**Unit 2:** Language and Culture
Unit 3: Families that Work	**Unit 3:** Exercise and Fitness
Unit 4: Staying in Business	**Unit 4:** Remarkable Researchers
Unit 5: Staying Healthy	**Unit 5:** Science and History
Unit 6: One of a Kind	**Unit 6:** Future Technology Today
Unit 7: Learning to Learn	
Unit 8: Play Time	
(Adelson-Goldstein with Howard, 2004, page iv)	(Smith and Mare, 2004, pages xi–xiii)

Action

With a classmate or colleague, compare the two tables of contents in Example 1. Then discuss the following questions.

1. What similarities and differences do you see in the themes?
2. What themes do you think would be of interest to beginning level readers? Rank the units in order of interest to beginning level readers.
3. If you were going to write a beginning level ESL or EFL book, how would you gather information on appropriate themes to include?

Teaching reading strategies and skills versus *testing* reading comprehension

One challenge that many teachers face is the struggle of balancing *teaching* learners effective **reading strategies** and skills and *testing* of reading comprehension. As L2 teachers, we want to make sure that our syllabus provides ample opportunities for explicit instruction on various reading strategies. We do not want to fall into the trap of developing a syllabus that mainly consists of reading passages following by reading comprehension questions. We want to engage the readers in discussions about the reading strategies that will help them become proficient readers and then provide opportunities for them to apply the strategies in their reading.

You may recall from Chapter 1 that strategies are defined as "the *conscious* actions that readers take to improve their **reading skills**. Strategies may be mental but observable, such as observing someone taking notes while reading to recall information better, or strategies may be mental and unobservable, such as thinking about what one already knows on a topic before reading a passage. Because strategies are conscious, there is active involvement of the reader in their selection and use" (page 10).

In Chapter Four of *Practical English Language Teaching*, I pointed out the importance of encouraging readers to transform their reading strategies into reading skills. Teachers should understand the differences in the terms *strategies* and *skills*. Strategies are the conscious actions that learners take to achieve desired goals or objectives, while skills are strategies that have become automatic. This characterization underscores the active role that readers play in strategic reading. As learners consciously learn and practice specific reading strategies, the strategies move from conscious to unconscious; from strategy to skill. Figure 1 provides a graphic representation of this concept.

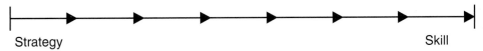

Strategy   Skill

Figure 1: Strategy-to-skill continuum

In a personal communication to me, PELT series editor David Nunan told me he makes a similar distinction between strategies and skills. He tells his students that strategies and skills are two sides of a coin. The strategy is inherent in the task, while the skill, once internalized and automated, is inherent in the language user. This analogy may also help you better understand the differences between strategies and skills.

For example, guessing the meaning of unknown vocabulary from context can be listed as both a strategy and a skill in reading texts. When a reader is first introduced to this concept and is practicing how to use context to guess the meaning of unfamiliar vocabulary, he is using a strategy. The use of the strategy is conscious during the learning and practice stages. As the ability to guess unfamiliar vocabulary from context becomes automatic, the reader moves from using a conscious strategy to using an unconscious skill. The use of the skill takes place outside the direct consciousness of the reader. The goal for explicit strategy instruction is to move readers from conscious control of reading strategies to unconscious use of reading skills.

When developing your reading syllabus, it is important to determine the role explicit teaching of strategies will play. Example 2 is the table of contents for another recently published reading textbook for beginning level readers. Notice that Chapters 1, 5, and 9 are entitled *Reading Skills and Strategies.* The author of this series obviously believes the explicit teaching of strategies is important. She has devoted 25 percent of the book to it. The other chapters in the book then provide practice of the skills and strategies explicitly taught.

Example 2

ReadSmart 1 High Beginning

Chapter 1: Reading Skills and Strategies
Chapter 2: Fire!
Chapter 3: The Extraordinary Shark
Chapter 4: All About Hair
Chapter 5: Reading Skills and Strategies
Chapter 6: Food on the Run
Chapter 7: Underground World
Chapter 8: Numbers, Numbers, Numbers
Chapter 9: Reading Skills and Strategies
Chapter 10: Along the Silk Road
Chapter 11: Hurray For Hollywood!
Chapter 12: Bridges

(Pavlik, 2004, pages iv–vii)

In Section 4 (pages 31–45), we will examine how these suggestions for syllabus design are incorporated into actual activities for teaching beginning level readers. But first, let's examine some basic principles that can guide the teaching of reading to beginning learners.

3. Principles for teaching reading to beginning learners

There are five principles I would like to draw your attention to as you prepare to teach reading to beginning proficiency level learners. The five principles are:

1. Select appropriate reading materials.
2. Balance bottom-up, top-down, and interactive reading instruction.
3. Explicitly teach reading strategies.
4. Focus attention on vocabulary development skills.
5. Provide both intensive and extensive reading instruction.

Let's consider each of these principles and how they can guide us in the teaching of reading.

1. Select appropriate reading materials.

Fifty years ago, Betts (1957) published *Foundations of Reading Instruction.* He gave what I consider to be the best instruction to teachers about selecting level-appropriate reading material. Although his guidelines were intended for teachers of reading to first language English speakers, I find his advice applicable for today's second language readers.

Betts outlined four levels of reading: basal level, instructional level, frustration level, and capacity level. Teachers should consider the goals of reading instruction and select passages that will achieve those goals. Let's take a quick look at each of Betts' levels.

Basal reading level

The basal reading level is reading at an independent level. A reader would be able to read the passage without assistance from a teacher with at least 90 percent comprehension.

This brings to mind Krashen's **input hypothesis** (1982). Krashen's input hypothesis suggests that second language acquisition is facilitated when learners receive input that is comprehensible. If learners are at a stage i, then acquisition takes place when they are exposed to "comprehensible input" that belongs to level $i + 1$. In other words, the input will be just a little above the learners' current ability level.

Using the $i + 1$ analogy, we can think of the basal reading level as being $i - 1$. At this level, we want the reading material to be easy for the reader.

We want to use easier material for pedagogical reasons. If our pedagogical goal is to help readers increase reading fluency, the reading material should be at an easier reading level so that the learners are not overwhelmed with difficult reading material. You want the reader to be able to accomplish the goal of reading fluently without the challenge of difficult material.

Instructional reading level

Betts' second level of reading material is called the instructional level, or what he also calls the teaching level. Readers should be able to understand 75 percent of what they read at this level. In terms of Krashen's input hypothesis, we can relate this to $i + 1$. The material for instructional reading should be just a bit above the current ability level of the reader. This level of reading material works well for vocabulary instruction. For example, if your pedagogical purpose is to teach readers how to use the context to guess the meaning of unfamiliar vocabulary words, then the difficulty level of the material should be just a bit above the ability level of the readers. In this way, the reader is challenged with new vocabulary. But because the reader should be able to understand the material 75 percent of the time, there will be enough context to help the reader guess the meanings of unfamiliar vocabulary.

Frustration reading level

The third level of appropriate reading material as outlined by Betts is called the frustration level. At this level, readers' comprehension is 50 percent or lower. There is so much new vocabulary and perhaps grammatical structures that it is difficult for the reader to understand. This level is one that we should avoid completely. Unfortunately in many classrooms around the world, the reading material is too challenging for the learners. Drawing on Krashen's input hypothesis, material at the frustration reading level would be $i + 2$, or 5, or 20. Material that is far above the level of the reader causes frustration and not opportunities for enjoyment or instruction.

Capacity reading level

The capacity level is what a learner can understand while listening to material read aloud by the teacher. At all levels of language proficiency, I see great value in the teacher reading aloud to learners in the classroom to develop capacity level reading abilities. Especially at the beginning levels of proficiency, reading aloud to the class and allowing them to simply listen provides a rich environment for improving reading. I have practiced this in two ways. Sometimes, I read aloud to my students while they only listen. Other times, I read aloud while the class follows silently in the text. As the readers listen, they get input on intonation, phrasing, and word clusters.

In terms of Krashen's input hypothesis, we can relate this to i. The material is right at the ability level of the reader. This level of reading material works well for reading strategy instruction. For example, if your pedagogical purpose is to teach readers how to identify the main ideas in a reading passage, then the difficulty level of the material should be at the ability level of the readers; not too easy and not too difficult. In this way, the reader can focus on the development of the strategy and not be overwhelmed with difficult reading material.

In addition to these four levels of reading material outlined by Betts, we should keep the interest level of the readers in mind. Find out what your students are interested in reading. What are their hobbies? What is an area they are interested in learning more about? By keeping student interest in mind, we can choose material that will help encourage an interest and desire to read.

Summary

The four levels that Betts outlines can be used for preparing materials at the appropriate pedagogical level for our students. I teach my students about these levels of texts and give them help in selecting appropriate reading material for their own reading outside of the classroom. I tell my students to select a book and then read one page, holding up a finger each time they see a word they do not know or understand. If they are selecting basal reading level material, for every 100 words, they should not have raised all ten fingers. This means that they understand at least 90 percent of the words and should find the book appropriate. If they are trying to select instructional level material, they should not have identified more than 25 words that they do not understand for every 100 words. If while looking for a book, the students find they do not understand 50 or more of the words out of 100, they have reached the frustration reading level. They should be encouraged to put the book down and find something else.

We also highlighted the importance of choosing material that is of interest to your students. Drawing upon their interests will encourage reading.

The selection of appropriate reading material is very important for the teacher. We want to make sure that the material that we are using helps us achieve our instructional goals and is not a roadblock in the development of good readers.

2. Balance bottom-up, top-down, and interactive reading instruction.

In Chapter 1, we discussed **bottom-up, top-down**, and **interactive reading** processes (pages 5–8). Recall that **bottom-up processing** consists of lower-level reading processes. In a bottom-up model, students start from the bottom (letters and sounds) to get to the top (comprehension). In **top-down processing**, the reader uses background knowledge, makes predictions, and searches the text to confirm or reject the predictions that are made. Within a top-down approach to reading, the teacher focuses on meaning-generating activities. The best readers in any language are those who use **interactive reading**, which integrates elements of both bottom-up and top-down reading. In the development of a reading syllabus, it is important to consider the balance that you will give to these processes.

Beginning level readers should be exposed to a strong bottom-up component. This is perhaps the greatest weakness in the development of many reading syllabi. Little or no attention is given to the explicit instruction of bottom-up reading. A guideline that you could follow in preparing a syllabus for beginning level readers is allocating 50 percent of your syllabus to teaching bottom-up skills, 30 percent to top-down skills, and 20 percent to interactive skills. With a strong foundation in bottom-up skills, beginning level readers will become more proficient readers more quickly.

Systematic phonics instruction is a bottom-up approach to reading that should be integrated into reading materials for beginning proficiency level readers. However, the reality is that most textbooks do not deal with phonics instruction. One series that has been specifically developed with phonics principles in mind is *Sam and Pat*, Books 1 and 2 (Hartel, Lowry, and Hendon, 2006). *Sam and Pat* is specifically written as a phonics-based series that uses a storyline to teach reading and writing skills at the low-beginning proficiency level.

Each book is structured with just over 20 lessons that introduce a phonics sequence to help beginning level readers become familiar with the sounds of English. For example, in Lesson 1 of Book 1, the consonants *s, m, p, t, f, g, c, d, f,* and *n* are introduced along with the short *a* vowel sound. The simple storyline is appropriate for adult learners of English. These books are one resource that can help teachers focus on the bottom-up skills necessary for developing effective reading skills.

There are also effective phonics programs that provide detailed teacher instruction as well as online learning support. Since much of the learning necessary for successful phonics skills is individual, the computer-based learning environment is a particularly good resource for English language teachers. One such program is *Reading Horizons: Discover Intensive Phonics for Yourself. Reading Horizons* consists of 30 lessons. The lessons divide the 42 sounds of English into four consonant sounds and one vowel sound per lesson and systematically introduce the letters by name and sound. Students then learn how to blend the consonant and vowel sounds. They then are taught **digraphs** and **diphthongs** followed by **special vowel sounds**.

Reading Horizons teaches beginning readers five phonetic skills for effectively decoding sounds in English. The five skills are:

1. When the vowel is followed by one guardian consonant and nothing more, the vowel will be short.
2. When the vowel is followed by two guardian consonants and nothing more, the vowel will be short.

3. When a vowel stands alone, it will be long.

4. Silent *e* makes the first vowel long.

5. When vowels are adjacent, the second vowel is silent and the first vowel is long.

In addition, *Reading Horizons* teaches two decoding skills:

1. If there is only one guardian consonant following the vowel, that consonant will move on to the next syllable.

2. When a vowel is followed by two guardian consonants, the consonants will split. The first consonant will stay in the first syllable and the second consonant will move on to the next syllable.

The program can be accomplished in the classroom with a trained teacher who understands the teaching methodology used by *Reading Horizons.* In addition to explicit classroom instruction, the lessons can be delivered via the computer. The computer program guides the students through the lessons and provides auditory as well as visual input for learning the phonics rules.

3. Explicitly teach reading strategies.

Strategy instruction is extremely important for readers, especially those at the beginning level of language proficiency. Nunan (1996, 1997) provides a good rationale for integrating explicit instruction of language learning strategies into the classroom curriculum. "[L]anguage classrooms should have a dual focus, not only teaching language content but also on developing learning processes as well" (Nunan, 1996, p. 41). The primary purpose of instruction is to raise learners' awareness of strategies and then allow each to select appropriate strategies to accomplish their learning goals.

In *Strategies for Success: A Practical Guide to Learning English* (2002), Brown provides a very practical guide, firmly based on the L2 strategy research, on how to approach the teaching of language learning strategies in the classroom. Teachers and learners are guided through the language learning strategy process in an effective and organized fashion.

Strategies for Success focuses on second language learners becoming aware of their individual learning styles, understanding the role of motivation, and setting clear learning goals, while also taking into account self-confidence, anxiety, and risk-taking for the non-native speaker. Brown introduces a concept of language-learning IQ building on Gardner's work in multiple intelligences. He encourages learners to be aware of the following seven intelligences: linguistic, logical-mathematical, spatial, bodily-kinesthetic, musical, interpersonal, and intrapersonal. Additional chapters focus on the role of one's first language and culture, as well as working by oneself and in small groups. Also, test-taking strategies are addressed.

In applying this principle of explicit strategy instruction with beginning level readers, one word of caution should be followed: Do not overwhelm the readers with too many strategies. Focus on five or six core strategies and give your readers multiple opportunities to practice them. Below is a list of appropriate reading strategies to consider teaching beginning level readers.

- Activate prior knowledge
- Ask questions
- Identify the main idea
- Make predictions
- Scan for specific information
- Skim for the main ideas

One suggestion is to post these strategies in your classroom so that you can refer to them often. Encourage your students to practice these strategies when reading passages in class and when doing outside reading. Ask your students to keep a reading journal and to respond to writing prompts that ask specifically about their development of these reading strategies. For example, I have students respond to the following journal prompts as they learn how to use reading strategies:

- Review the list of strategies on our class poster. Which ones have you used in class today? Give a specific example of how you used one.
- In today's class, we practiced the reading strategy of asking questions. What questions did you specifically ask as we read today's text?

Following these ideas will help you to implement this principle in your teaching of reading.

4. Focus attention on vocabulary development skills.

Beginning level readers need a clear focus on vocabulary-development skills. Readers at this level consider their lack of vocabulary to be their greatest challenge. There are very simple steps that you can take in order to assure that vocabulary development happens in an organized fashion.

First, review the General Service List (GSL) of the 1,000 and 2,000 most frequently used words in English. A useful copy of the list can be found at the personal website of ESL professor John Bauman, http://jbauman.com/gsl.html. On this site, the actual words with their frequency numbers are provided. These are high-frequency words that beginning level readers should be familiar with.

Second, select words from the GSL and teach readers the other words from that word family. Two examples may be helpful. *Reflect* is the 925th most frequent word in English. *Reflect* is a verb. *Reflection* is the noun in this word family. *Reflectively* is the adverb, and *reflective* is the adjective. Another example comes from word 1142 in the frequency list: *friendly*. Teach your students that *friendly* is an adjective. This is a good adjective to teach because it ends in *−ly* and students are usually taught that words that end in *−ly* are adverbs. The noun in the word family is *friend*. *Friendship* is another noun.

Befriend is the verb in the word family. As you teach readers word families, their vocabulary skills will grow.

Third, teach synonyms of your target word. The synonyms extend the vocabulary beyond the word family and help the learners identify additional vocabulary. Appropriate synonyms for *friendly* include *welcoming, gracious, forthcoming, responsive,* and *sociable.* You see how teaching the synonyms builds vocabulary?

Finally, teach antonyms of your target word. Again, this practice extends vocabulary instruction beyond the target word and the word family. Antonyms of *friendly* include *unfriendly, hostile, uncordial,* and *unneighborly.* Notice the multiple examples of antonyms that use the prefix *un-.* If this prefix has not already been studied as part of word-analysis skills, now would be a good time to teach it.

For beginning level readers, selecting words from the General Service List is an appropriate way to focus attention on vocabulary-development skills.

5. Provide both intensive and extensive reading instruction.

The final principle for teaching reading to beginning readers directs our attention to teaching both **intensive** and **extensive reading**. In Chapter 1 (pages 8–10), I noted that intensive reading provides the opportunity to teach a particular reading skill and then give direct practice in that skill. Extensive reading provides an opportunity to read longer texts.

Textbooks written for classroom instruction will focus on intensive reading instruction. The challenge is designing a reading program that links both intensive reading instruction with extensive reading. Very few language programs are designed in such a way as to provide the explicit link between the two.

Action

Choose a textbook that you would like to use (or have used) for intensive reading instruction. Then identify how learners can practice the same reading skills through extensive reading.

Share your ideas with a classmate or colleague.

An example of integrating both intensive and extensive reading is given on pages 45–47 in Section 5, Reading inside and outside of the classroom.

4. Tasks and materials

In this section, I will provide examples that demonstrate a range of tasks and activities you can use to teach reading to beginning level readers. The examples provided are not intended to represent all possible activity types, but rather to give you ideas that you can use in your own classrooms. We will examine four categories of useful tasks for beginning readers.

1. Activation of background knowledge
2. Vocabulary instruction
3. Explicit strategy instruction
4. Building reading fluency

1. Activation of background knowledge

Prior to engaging learners in the reading process, it is important to activate their prior knowledge on the topic of the reading. Good readers connect new information that they are learning from their reading to what they already know. By making the connection, our comprehension increases. It is also important to recognize that you might have to *build* background knowledge. Readers might not have the necessary background to be successful in reading a passage. If students are reading about a new concept that is not part of their culture, they will need help in building knowledge. For example, Pritchard (1990) conducted an interesting study in which he asked readers to read about a funeral based on their local tradition and the tradition in the United States. One outcome of his research was that our cultural knowledge can influence our comprehension. Therefore, if you were going to ask students to read a text that included references to a funeral in the United States, you might need to both activate prior knowledge about funerals in the students' home countries as well as build knowledge about funerals in the U.S. You can facilitate comprehension by building a simple foundation from which students can continue to learn as they read.

Reflection

On the following pages are three examples from reading textbooks designed for beginning level learners. The examples all focus on preparing the readers to draw on what they already know in order to read successfully.

As you review each example, notice:

- how readers are encouraged to draw upon what they already know.
- whether you think the activity successfully prepares the learners to read.
- if there are any questions in these background activation activities for which readers may not have an answer.

Share your ideas with a classmate or colleague.

Example 3

Harry Potter

Before You Read

Answer the following questions.

1. Do you know who the person in the picture is? What do you know about her?

   _____

   _____

2. Have you read any Harry Potter books, or seen the movies? What did you think of them?

   _____

   _____

3. Who is the best-selling writer in your country? Have you read any of his or her books? If yes, what did you think of them?

   _____

   _____

Target Vocabulary

Match each word with the best meaning.

1. _____ publish   a. room for living in a building or house
2. _____ translate   b. get money by working
3. _____ earn   c. print and sell books, magazines, or newspapers
4. _____ afford   d. popular, or making a lot of money
5. _____ apartment   e. to have enough money to be able to buy something
6. _____ successful   f. change from one language to another

Reading Advantage 1, 2nd ed., (Malarcher, 2004, page 9)

Example 4

You are going to read three texts about clothes. First, answer the questions in the boxes.

Dressing for success

This magazine article describes what you should wear to a job interview and the effect of clothing on getting a job.

1. What do a person's clothes tell you about that person?
2. What do you think a young person should wear to a job interview? Why?

Casual dress in the workplace

Should people be allowed to dress casually at work? Find out about the trend toward casual dress at work and what people think about it.

1. What types of workers can dress casually at work? Why?
2. For which jobs do people have to wear suits or conservative clothes? What image do conservative clothes give?

T-shirts out; uniforms in

This newspaper article outlines some of the benefits of school uniforms.

1. Did/do you wear a uniform in school? Why do you think school uniforms are used around the world?
2. Which professions require employees to wear uniforms at work? Why do you think they have to wear uniforms?

Vocabulary

Find out the meanings of the words in *italics*. Then answer the questions about the people in the picture.

1. Which people are wearing *casual* clothes?
2. Which person is wearing the most *conservative* clothes?
3. Which person is wearing the most *stylish* clothes?
4. Which people are wearing an *outfit*?
5. Which person is most interested in *fashion*?
6. Which person is the most *dressed up*?
7. Which person *dresses* most like you?

Alison   David   Serena   Rick

Strategic Reading 1 (Richards and Eckstut-Didier, 2003, page 41)

Example 5

Staying Healthy

In this unit you will:

- read about the ways people in the U.S. stay healthy
- learn how to understand vocabulary in context

WHAT DO YOU KNOW ABOUT STAYING HEALTHY?

A. Look at the information in the medical records. With a partner, decide who is healthier, Chad or Sam. Why? Discuss your responses with your classmates.

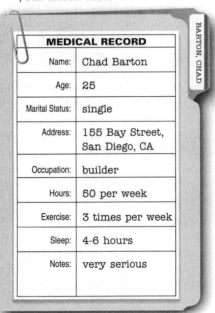

MEDICAL RECORD	
Name:	Chad Barton
Age:	25
Marital Status:	single
Address:	155 Bay Street, San Diego, CA
Occupation:	builder
Hours:	50 per week
Exercise:	3 times per week
Sleep:	4-6 hours
Notes:	very serious

BARTON, CHAD

MEDICAL RECORD	
Name:	Sam Hinton
Age:	27
Marital Status:	married
Address:	645 10th Street Brooklyn, NY
Occupation:	college professor
Hours:	40 per week
Exercise:	walks dog
Sleep:	6-8 hours
Notes:	good sense of humor

HINTON, SAM

B. Which of the following things do you do to stay healthy? Mark your answers with a check (✓). Discuss your responses with your classmates.

___ drink tea	___ drink water	___ eat fruit and vegetables
___ exercise	___ sleep well	___ take time to relax
___ take vitamins	___ other _____	

Read and Reflect 1 (Adelson-Goldstein and Howard, 2004, page 57)

The purpose of the activation of background knowledge is to prepare the reader for the material they will find in the text. Examples 3–5 do this by getting the reader to think about what they already know and by asking questions to get readers thinking.

2. Vocabulary instruction

Recall the four suggestions given in the previous section on principles related to vocabulary instruction: (1) teach high-frequency words, (2) teach word families, (3) teach synonyms, and (4) teach antonyms. On pages 37–39 are three excerpts from reading textbooks that focus on vocabulary instruction.

Action

See how the four principles are implemented in these textbooks. Use the chart below to help you as you look at the three excerpts. Place a check mark in the box that correctly illustrates a vocabulary instruction principle. After completing this Action Box, check your answers on page 54 at the end of this chapter.

	Teach high-frequency words	Teach word families	Teach synonyms	Teach antonyms
NorthStar Basic/Low Intermediate, p. 46				
Read and Reflect 1, p. 6				
ACTIVE Skills for Reading, Intro level, p. 57				

Example 6

1 *The sentences below do not make sense. Replace the underlined word or phrase with the antonym (or opposite of that word) from the box so the sentences make sense.*

arrested	completely	fake	nervous
casual	counterfeit	improved	prevent

1. When I bought the jeans, he told me they were Levi's. But when I got home,
   I saw that the Levi's name was not on the pocket. These were <u>real</u> Levi's
   counterfeit
   jeans.

2. Look at this bill. The ink is almost brown, not green. The paper feels like
   regular computer paper, not money. This must be the work of a <u>professional</u>
   counterfeiter.

3. The police officer took the woman by the arms, put her in the police car, and
   took her to the police station. He <u>set</u> her <u>free</u>.

4. Look at her diamond necklace. I can see scratch marks. It doesn't shine in
   the light. I think it's <u>real</u>.

5. His legs were shaking. His heart was going very fast. His lips were dry. He
   felt very <u>relaxed</u> as he gave the bank the counterfeit money.

6. The fire destroyed everything in the house. Everything that mattered to the
   family—the photos, the important papers, the furniture—was <u>not at all</u>
   destroyed.

7. Her English has <u>gotten worse</u>. She speaks more quickly and more smoothly.
   Her pronunciation is much better. And she seems more comfortable talking
   in English.

NorthStar Basic/Low Intermediate (Haugnes and Maher, 2004, page 46)

Example 7

WORK WITH THE VOCABULARY

A. Choose the word or phrase that has a meaning similar to the underlined word or phrase in the sentence. Look back at the article on page 4 to check your answers.

1. Some students become <u>extremely</u> anxious before a social event.

   a. less
   b. more
   c. very

2. They <u>suffer from</u> social anxiety.

   a. dislike
   b. have symptoms of
   c. are free from

3. They often feel that they can't <u>fit in with</u> any social group.

   a. be a part of
   b. focus on
   c. suffer from

4. Sometimes <u>academic challenges</u> can be a problem.

   a. parties
   b. difficult schoolwork
   c. club meetings

5. With help from counselors, students can <u>eliminate</u> their social anxiety.

   a. dislike
   b. find
   c. end

6. Counselors can show these students different <u>techniques</u> to fight social anxiety.

   a. ways
   b. breathing
   c. roads

B. Match each statement to the action it describes.

STATEMENT	ACTION
_d_ 1. "Your essay is very interesting."	a. experiencing social anxiety
___ 2. "Sara, this is Paul. Paul, this is Sara."	b. making an introduction
___ 3. "It's a nice day, isn't it?"	c. asking for an opinion
___ 4. "What if nobody talks to me in class?"	d. giving feedback
___ 5. "Do you think this is a good class?"	e. making small talk

Read and Reflect 1 (Adelson-Goldstein with Howard, 2004, p. 6)

Example 8

A Read the paragraph below. Find the missing parts of speech for each word family. Add the words to the chart.

Vocabulary Skill:
Word Families

Nouns	Verbs	Adjectives
competition ___ ___	___	competitive
___	win ___ (past tense)	___

In this chapter, you learned the word "competitive." In Chapter 1, you read the word "compete." These words are in the same "word family." You can build your vocabulary by learning word families.

> Every year, my high school has a spelling **competition**. Students from different grades compete against each other for first prize: $5,000! This year, my friend Jon entered . . . and he won! At the end, Jon's competitor was a girl named Angie. The winning word was *sarcophagus*. After Jon spelled it, everyone was quiet. Then the teacher said, "Congratulations. You're this year's winner!"

B Complete the sentences below with the correct word from the chart in A.

1 Leo is so _____! He always wants to _____.
2 In the swimming race, Bill's _____ was a boy named James.
3 Here's my lottery ticket. What are the _____ numbers?
4 There are five skaters in this year's ice-skating _____.

ACTIVE Skills for Reading, Intro level (Anderson, 2007, page 57)

3. Explicit strategy instruction

Strategy instruction is most effective when it is explicitly taught and successfully integrated into the materials. Many language teaching programs have prepared strategy modules to help readers. The disadvantage of such separate modules is that readers often do not make the direct connection between the reading strategy being taught and actual reading.

We will examine three examples of reading textbooks that explicitly teach reading strategies in effective ways.

ReadSmart 1 does a particularly good job at explicit strategy instruction. In *ReadSmart 1*, intended for high beginning proficiency readers, there are three Reading Skills and Strategies chapters integrated throughout the book. Notice in Example 9 on the following page that the chapter is divided into two parts: Comprehension Strategies and Vocabulary Strategies. The section

Comprehension Strategies is broken into three sections: Prepare, Read, and Remember. The chapter gives beginning level readers explicit instruction on various strategies that can then be practiced in the upcoming chapters.

Example 9

Overview of the Strategies

PART 1

Comprehension Strategies

Prepare
- Making Predictions about the Text
- Exploring What You Already Know
- Asking Questions about the Text

Read
- Marking the Text
- Reading More than Once
- Using Connectors (Personal Pronouns) to Follow Ideas
- Using Signal Words to Predict Ideas

Remember
- Using Pictures

PART 2

Vocabulary Strategies
- Deciding Which Words Are Important
- Looking for Internal Definitions
- Using Synonyms, Antonyms, and Restatements

ReadSmart 1 (Pavlik, 2004, page 9)

ACTIVE Skills for Reading is another textbook series that effectively integrates the explicit teaching of reading strategies into the material. Each chapter addresses a specific reading strategy. In Unit 7, Chapter 1, the target reading strategy is *Recognizing Sequence of Events*. Readers receive an explanation of the strategy and then have an opportunity to practice it.

Example 10

Reading Skill:
Recognizing
Sequence of Events

In this passage, information is listed in the order that events happened. The sequence is shown with dates and a variety of words and phrases: "first," "in A.D. 972," "a few years later," "around the year 988," "in the years that followed," etc. These words make the order of events very clear for the reader.

A Without looking at the passage on the next page, put the events in the time line below in the correct order (1–7). Circle the words that helped you choose the correct order. Compare your answers with a partner.

University Time Line

	Then, leaders of the city thought of the idea for a school for higher learning.
	Scholars from around the world came to the university to study and do research.
	One of the first courses taught there was law.
1	The university was first built as a mosque in A.D. 972.
	The mosque was used as a meeting place for teachers.
	After that, Al-Azhar University was started.
	Today, the university is still important.

B Quickly skim the reading passage on the next page. Compare the events in the reading with the order of events in your time line above.

C Read the passage again and answer the questions that follow.

ACTIVE Skills for Reading, Book 1, 2nd ed. (Anderson, 2007, page 88)

Example 11 on the following page is drawn from *Read and Reflect 1.* Finding clues in context is the reading skill taught in Unit 5. Notice that the readers are provided with explicit instruction and then have the opportunity to practice.

Example 11

BUILDING READING SKILLS: Finding Clues in Context

Finding clues in context means getting information about the meaning of important words in a text by looking at the sentences nearby. You will usually find the clues in the same sentence or paragraph as the important words. These clues can be synonyms (similar words), definitions, examples, or contrasts (opposite ideas or words).

Practice Finding Clues in Context

Read the paragraph and think about the meanings of the underlined words. Use context clues to answer the questions below.

> Many people get <u>migraines</u>. These headaches make them very ill. To help their patients, doctors are studying the <u>causes</u> of migraines. They know there are many reasons for these headaches. <u>Some things in the environment</u> can cause a migraine. Poor air quality, lights, or too much noise in homes and workplaces can result in a migraine attack. Some doctors believe, however, that the <u>emotional</u> (not the physical) <u>environment</u> is a more likely cause of an attack.

1. What is a migraine? (Look for a synonym.)

2. What does *causes* mean? (Look for the definition.)

3. What are *things in the environment*? (Look for examples.)

4. What do you think the *emotional environment* is? (Look for a contrast clue.)

Use Your Reading Skills

A. Preview the introductory material, the title, and the headings of the article on page 60. Discuss these questions with your classmates.

1. What is the topic of this article?

2. What do you know about this topic?

B. As you read the article on page 60, highlight the clues that tell you the meanings of these words. Then write the clues on the lines below.

1. quack _____

2. quick fix _____

3. urban population _____

4. opium _____

5. radium _____

6. illegal _____

Read and Reflect 1 (Adelson-Goldstein with Howard, 2004, page 59)

There are many ways to explicitly teach reading strategies to beginning level readers. Given examples 9–11, what are four reading strategies you would focus on with beginning level readers? Why?

Share your ideas with a classmate or colleague.

4. Building reading fluency

Very few reading materials actually focus on the development of **reading fluency**. Recall that reading fluency is defined as reading at an adequate rate with adequate comprehension. *Reading Power* and *ACTIVE Skills for Reading* are the exceptions. These reading series explicitly focus on the development of fluency.

Part 4 of *Reading Power* reviews with the readers why reading faster is a skill that should be developed. Example 12 shows the three steps for how to read faster that are taught to the readers.

Example 12

Step 1: Check your reading habits. The authors tell the readers to be aware of bad reading habits that may slow down their reading. For example, trying to pronounce each word as you read slows you down.

Step 2: Skip over unknown words. A very good exercise is provided that has a paragraph with words that are actually missing. Comprehension questions follow that show the reader that even when they do not have all of the words in a passage they can still understand.

Step 3: Practice reading faster by timing yourself. The authors explain to readers that if they are reading slower than 200 words per minute that they are reading word by word. They are encouraged to push themselves to read faster.

Reading Power 3rd ed. (Mikulecky and Jeffries, 2005, pages 179–181)

ACTIVE Skills for Reading, Book 1, 2nd ed. (2007) focuses on the development of reading fluency in four review units. Each review unit consists of three reading passages and begins with instruction of a specific reading fluency strategy. Strategies such as skipping unknown words, SQ3R (Survey, Question, Read, Review, Recite), and KWL (What do I already Know about this topic?, What do I Want to learn as I read?, and What did I Learn while reading?) are taught to the readers. Teachers are provided with four explicit reading fluency activities that can be used to develop reading fluency: rate buildup reading, repeated reading, class-paced reading, and self-paced reading. One of these activities is given in Example 13.

Example 13

Fluency Strategy: *SQ3R*

SQ3R is a simple way to help you be a better, more fluent reader and to increase your reading comprehension. SQ3R stands for **S**urvey, **Q**uestion, **R**ead, **R**eview, **R**ecite.

Survey

Survey is similar to the A in the ACTIVE approach to reading; Activate prior knowledge. When you survey, you prepare yourself by skimming quickly through the text you will read. You read the title, the headings, and the first sentence in each section of the passage. You look for and read words that are written in **bold** or *italic*. Look at any pictures and read any captions. Through the survey you prepare yourself to read.

Look below at extracts from the passage on the next page, "The 'Freshman Fifteen,'" then go on to the Question section.

The "Freshman Fifteen"
You may not have heard the words "freshman fifteen" before, but they are very important for students who are entering university. A freshman is a first-year college student.

Mistakes choosing food

Eating right

Question

After the survey, but before you read, ask yourself **questions**. "What do I want to learn as I read?"

Based on your survey of "The 'Freshman Fifteen,'" write two or three questions that you hope to answer as you read.

1 _____

2 _____

3 _____

Read

Following the survey and question stage of SQ3R you **read**. You focus on comprehending the material. You move your eyes fluently through the material.

Read "The 'Freshman Fifteen.'" As you read, keep in mind the 12 tips on pages 8 and 9. By combining those tips and SQ3R you will improve your reading fluency.

ACTIVE Skills for Reading, Book 1, 2nd ed. (Anderson, 2007, page 41)

Reflection

Have you found second-language reading materials that explicitly focus on the development of reading fluency? What do you think about the examples that have been provided here? Which examples would you be most likely to use in your own reading classroom? Why? What else can you do to improve reading fluency of the students you work with or might work with?

Share your ideas with a classmate or colleague.

5. Reading inside and outside of the classroom

Inside the classroom, reading instruction should focus on the explicit development of reading skills and comprehension skills of beginning level readers. There are a wide variety of textbooks available from commercial publishers that can meet the needs of most English language programs around the world. Below is a list of appropriate titles intended for readers at beginning levels of language proficiency.

> *ACTIVE Skills for Reading*, Introductory level, Thomson ELT
> *ACTIVE Skills for Reading*, 2nd edition, Book 1, Thomson ELT
> *NorthStar Reading and Writing*, Basic/Low intermediate, Longman
> *On Location 1: Reading and Writing for Success in the Content Areas*, McGraw-Hill
> *Quest Intro Reading and Writing*, McGraw-Hill
> *Quest 1 Reading and Writing*, McGraw-Hill
> *Read and Reflect*, Oxford University Press
> *Read On 1*, McGraw-Hill
> *Reading Advantage 1*, 2nd edition, Thomson ELT
> *ReadSmart 1*, McGraw-Hill
> *Strategic Reading 1*, Cambridge University Press
> *Themes for Today*, 2nd edition, Thomson ELT

Take advantage of the publisher's website to review the material. Contact the publisher's representative in your area. Identify a text that meets the goals of your program.

Outside of the classroom, teachers can encourage students to be engaged in extensive reading. Teachers have excellent resources available from the commercial publishing companies. In the Action box on page 46 are websites that link you to appropriate extensive reading book ideas.

Cambridge English Readers
   www.cambridge.org/elt/catalogue/
Macmillan Readers
   www.macmillanenglish.com/readers/
Penguin Readers
   www.penguinreaders.com/

Visit these websites and review the extensive reading materials. Do you think that you would (or could) use any of these books for students to read outside of the classroom? Why or why not?

Share your answers with a classmate or colleague.

Keep in mind Figure 5 from Chapter 1 (page 9). Successful reading programs have an explicit connection between in-class and out-of-class reading. The skills that you are teaching in class can be connected to practice opportunities outside of class. Let me provide an example.

In *ACTIVE Skills for Reading*, Book 1, 2nd edition, Unit 7, the title of Chapter 1 is "The Oldest University in the World." The reading skill that is taught in this chapter is *Recognizing Sequence of Events*. The reading skill is taught with the following explanation:

> In this passage, information is listed in the order that events happened. The sequence is shown with dates and a variety of words and phrases: "first," "in A.D. 972," "a few years later," "around the year 988," "in the years that followed," etc. These words make the order of events very clear for the reader. (page 88)

Students are then given an opportunity to practice the skill with the reading "The Oldest University in the World." This constitutes the intensive reading instruction.

For extensive reading using the same skill, students can be assigned to read from the following sources:

> *Sacajawea: Wilderness Guide*
> *Sacagawea* (Kids Discover)
> *Lewis & Clark* (Kids Discover)

These titles provide both narrative (*Sacajawea: Wilderness Guide*) and expository (*Sacagawea and Lewis & Clark*) reading practice where there are natural opportunities to practice the reading skill of recognizing the sequence of events. These extensive reading passages provide timelines and maps of Sacagawea's travels with Lewis and Clark. Although the reading passage from *ACTIVE Skills for Reading* is different from the extensive reading passages, the focus on the reading skills is the objective. Finding the connections among the passages with the reading skill helps the readers to understand the importance of developing their reading skills.

6. Assessing beginning readers

Assessment is an essential component of any classroom. Good teachers need to be aware of basic principles of assessment. This knowledge can help them to be better teachers. It is beyond the scope of this chapter to teach these basic principles. I refer you to Chapter 15 of *Practical English Language Teaching* (Nunan, 2003), Classroom-based Assessment by Geoff Brindley. That chapter outlines basic principles that can guide teachers to a deeper understanding of the role of assessment in the classroom.

In this section, we will review five areas of assessment that teachers should be aware of and, in particular, identify how these principles can be applied with beginning level readers. The five areas include: placement tests, diagnostic tests, progress tests, achievement tests, and learner self-assessment.

Placement tests

The program in which you teach should have a **placement test** that places learners into classes. Most programs will place learners by levels of language proficiency. These groupings by level may still be quite broad. There can be a range of abilities even within a class of beginning level learners. If there is a reading component to the placement test, valuable information is available to you. Review the scores of each of the students. Calculate the average score. Look at how large the range of scores is of those who have taken the placement test. The smaller the range of scores, the more homogeneous your class will be. The wider the range of scores, the more heterogeneous your class will be.

Diagnostic tests

After a placement test is given, the next appropriate test to administer is a **diagnostic test**. Diagnostic tests elicit more specific information than do placement tests because diagnostic tests focus on the strengths and weaknesses of students at a particular level (e.g., beginners). Diagnostic tests provide input to you as a teacher on what your students already know how to do and what they still need to learn.

One diagnostic tool that I consistently use in the reading classroom is the Survey of Reading Strategies (SORS) that was introduced in Chapter 1 (page 11). The results of that survey give me as well as the readers a general overview of reading strategies with which they are familiar. I gather all of the individual scores on the SORS and create a class average. I present the class averages to the readers on a graph and help them see how we can use the results of the survey to make improvements in the development of our reading skills. For example, the graph below shows the class averages on the SORS from a recent class I taught. Note that the graph divides the scores into high, medium, and low. These score indicate frequency of strategy use. For this recent class, the overall SORS average was 2.6, a medium frequency use. The global reading strategy frequency was 3.0 (medium), the problem solving strategy frequency was 3.7 (high), and the support strategy frequency was 2.0 (low). With these results, I developed a syllabus to teach more support strategies and global reading strategies as students continued to strengthen their problem-solving strategies.

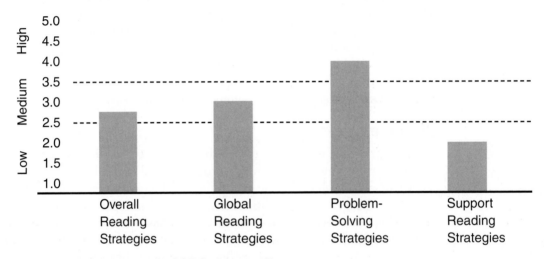

Figure 2: sample SORS class profile

Progress tests

Take advantage of opportunities to evaluate the progress of your students during instruction to see how well they are mastering the reading skills that you are teaching. It is important to provide the readers with input on the improvements they are making as they read. **Progress tests** can focus on both reading comprehension improvements, reading fluency improvements, and/or improvements in specific reading skills.

One resource that I am aware of that helps teachers prepare progress tests is a computer program, *ExamView. ExamView* or a similar program is provided by publishing companies to accompany a particular reading series. For example, *ExamView* accompanies *ACTIVE Skills for Reading.* When the computer disk is loaded, you are asked which book you are using (Intro, Book 1, 2, 3, or 4) and then which unit from the book you want to test. You are then able to select the number and type of question you would like to include on the progress test. Teachers can select from multiple-choice, true/false, or short-answer questions. The program has a data bank of additional reading passages and test questions. Based on the selections you make in the program, you can create a progress test in less than five minutes. Teachers can add additional questions to the test and even edit questions that are part of the test bank. This is a very easy way for teachers to prepare a progress test.

Achievement tests

Achievement tests provide input on how well the students are meeting the goals of your class. At the end of the course you can administer an achievement test to provide input to you and to program administrators on how well the students did during the course. The data from achievement tests is valuable in discovering the types of changes you need to make in your reading program the next time it is offered. If your textbook is supported with a program like *ExamView* or *EZ Test*, you can create your end-of-course achievement test easily. Many programs may have their own achievement tests that are administered to students in the program. In other programs, teachers prepare their own achievement tests. Keep in mind that the goal of administering an achievement test is to verify that students are mastering the skills taught your reading class.

Reflection

Are you familiar with each of the assessment types described above? If you are currently teaching a reading class, how do you use these assessments in your program? If you are not teaching, how do you think you will use them?

Share your ideas with a classmate or colleague.

Learner self-assessment

In addition to the types of tests described above, training learners in self-assessment of their own skills is a very important part of our teaching responsibilities. Let me share an example of one way I have implemented a self-assessment procedure.

When I administer a test (diagnostic, progress, or achievement), I ask the students to review their performance on each of the test items. Let's assume that I have just administered a midterm exam on which I assessed students on the following reading skills: scanning, skimming for the main idea, predicting, identifying the meaning of unknown vocabulary in context, and identifying main ideas. While they still have their copy of the test booklet, I give them a handout like the one on page 50 and ask them to complete Parts A, B, and C.

Example 14

Name: _____

Self-Assessment of Performance on the Midterm Exam

Part A

How do you think your score on this midterm exam will compare with that of other students in the class?

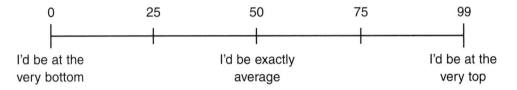

| 0 | 25 | 50 | 75 | 99 |

I'd be at the
very bottom

I'd be exactly
average

I'd be at the
very top

Part B

Go back over *each* of the questions on this quiz and provide a self-assessment of your
performance. How well do you think you did on *each* item?

Item	Do you believe you will receive *full* credit for your response on this item? Yes No I'm not sure (circle one)		
Section 1. Scanning			
1.	Yes	No	I'm not sure
2.	Yes	No	I'm not sure
3.	Yes	No	I'm not sure
4.	Yes	No	I'm not sure
5.	Yes	No	I'm not sure
Section 2. Skimming for the Main Idea			
6.	Yes	No	I'm not sure
7.	Yes	No	I'm not sure
8.	Yes	No	I'm not sure
9.	Yes	No	I'm not sure
10.	Yes	No	I'm not sure

Section 3. Predicting			
11.	Yes	No	I'm not sure
12.	Yes	No	I'm not sure
13.	Yes	No	I'm not sure
14.	Yes	No	I'm not sure
15.	Yes	No	I'm not sure
Section 4. Identifying the Meaning of Unknown Vocabulary in Context			
16.	Yes	No	I'm not sure
17.	Yes	No	I'm not sure
18.	Yes	No	I'm not sure
19.	Yes	No	I'm not sure
20.	Yes	No	I'm not sure
Section 5. Identifying Main Ideas			
21.	Yes	No	I'm not sure
22.	Yes	No	I'm not sure
23.	Yes	No	I'm not sure
24.	Yes	No	I'm not sure
25.	Yes	No	I'm not sure

Part C

There are a total of 25 points on this test. What do you estimate will be your score?

_____ of the 25 points

After the exam is corrected, I return it to the students along with the self-assessment sheet. I then ask them to complete Part D of the form.

> **Example 15**
>
> **Part D** (to be completed after receiving the results of the test)
>
> My actual score was _____ / 25 points
>
> I _____ my score on this test.
>
>   A. overestimated (I estimated my score would be higher.)
>
>   B. correctly estimated
>
>   C. underestimated (I estimated my score would be lower.)
>
> In preparation for the next test, I will do the following things to improve my score:
>
> _____
>
> _____

This self-assessment activity provides explicit practice for the students in being more aware of what they are doing as readers. The students begin to make connections between the questions on the test and their ability to assess their skills. They also become more aware of their strengths and weaknesses as readers.

Action

Develop a self-assessment tool that you could use with a group of readers based on a diagnostic, progress, or achievement test.

Share your self-assessment tool with a classmate or colleague.

7. Conclusion

In this chapter, we have focused our attention on the development of reading skills for readers at the beginning level of language proficiency. We have considered how reading is typically taught to learners at beginning levels. Then we explored the differences between teaching reading and testing reading comprehension. We have identified reading strategies appropriate for beginning level readers as well as how to recognize principles of teaching beginning level readers. We concluded the chapter explaining five different tools for assessment: placement tests, diagnostic tests, progress tests, achievement tests, and learner self-assessment. The concepts outlined here will help you meet the reading needs of beginning level learners.

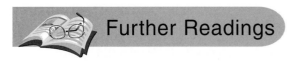

Further Readings

Bamford, J. and R.R. Day. 2004. (Eds.) *Extensive Reading Activities for Teaching Language.* Cambridge, UK: Cambridge University Press.

This book is a very useful resource for identifying activities that can be used in extensive reading.

Mokhtari, K. and Sheorey, R. (eds.) 2008. *Reading Strategies of First- and Second-language Learners: See how they read.* Norwood, MA: Christopher-Gordon Publishers.

Mokhtari and Sheorey address the strategy-to-skill (conscious to unconscious) continuum discussed in this chapter. They also give techniques for explicit teaching of reading strategies.

Helpful Websites

Reading Horizons (www.readinghorizons.com/)

Reading Horizons provides background information on the systematic phonics program discussed in this chapter.

About the General Service List (http://jbauman.com/aboutgsl.html)

John Bauman's personal site gives a complete version of the GSL, as well as background information on the list and its development.

Cambridge English Readers (http://www.cambridge.org/elt/catalogue/)
Macmillan Readers (http://www.macmillanenglish.com/readers)
Penguin Readers (http://www.penguinreaders.com)

These three publishers' sites give a good overview of the extensive reading materials currently on the market.

References

Anderson, N.J. 2003. Reading. In D. Nunan (Ed.) *Practical English Language Teaching* (pp. 67–86). New York, NY: McGraw Hill.

Anderson, N.J. 2004. Metacognitive Reading Strategy Awareness of ESL and EFL Learners. *The CATESOL Journal, 16I (1), 1–17.*

Betts, E.A. 1957. *Foundations of Reading Instruction: With emphasis on differentiated guidance.* New York, NY: American Book Company.

Brindley, G. 2003. Classroom-based Assessment. In D. Nunan (Ed.) *Practical English Language Teaching* (pp. 309–328). New York: McGraw Hill.

Brown, H.D. 2002. *Strategies for Success: A Practical Guide to Learning English.* White Plains, NY: Longman.

Council of Europe. 2001. *Common European Framework of Reference for Languages: Learning, Teaching, Assessment.* Cambridge, UK: Cambridge University Press.

Hartel, J., B. Lowry, and W. Hendon. 2006. *Sam and Pat,* Book 1: Beginning reading and writing. Boston, MA: Thomson.

Hartel, J., B. Lowry, and W. Hendon. 2006. *Sam and Pat,* Book 2: Beginning reading and writing. Boston, MA: Thomson.

Jassem, K. (n.d.). *Sacajawea: Wilderness guide.* Mahwah, NJ: Troll Associates.

Kids Discover (n.d.). *Lewis & Clark.* New York, NY: Kids Discover.

Kids Discover (n.d.). *Lincoln.* New York, NY: Kids Discover.

Kids Discover (n.d.). *Sacagawea.* New York, NY: Kids Discover.

Krashen, S.D. 1982. *Principles and Practice of Second Language Acquisition.* Oxford, UK: Pergamon.

Nunan, D. 1996. Learner Strategy Training in the Classroom: An action research study. *TESOL Journal, 6,* 35–41.

Nunan, D. 1997. Does Learner Training Make a Difference? *Lenguas Modernas, 24,* 123–142.

Pritchard, R. 1990. The Effects of Cultural Schemata on Reading Processing Strategies. *Reading Research Quarterly, 25,* 273–295.

Answer Key for Action Box on page 36.

	Teach high-frequency words	Teach word families	Teach synonyms	Teach antonyms
NorthStar Basic/Low Intermediate, p. 46	✓			✓
Read and Reflect 1, p. 6	✓		✓	
ACTIVE Skills for Reading, Intro level, p. ??	✓	✓		

Chapter **Three**

Reading for intermediate level learners

Goals

At the end of this chapter, you should be able to:

✔ **describe** what makes an intermediate level reader different from a beginning level reader.

✔ **explain** the learning/reading continuum and what factors teachers should consider when teaching intermediate level readers.

✔ **overcome** the "intermediate level slump."

✔ **identify** essential elements of reading syllabus design for intermediate level readers.

✔ **recognize** principles of teaching intermediate level readers.

✔ **identify** reading strategies appropriate for intermediate level readers.

✔ **create** an achievement test to measure reading progress.

1. Introduction

In Chapter 2, I explained that in the *Practical English Language Teaching* series, the level of language proficiency (beginning, intermediate, and advanced) is used as the organizing framework. In this chapter, we will address the issues dealing with intermediate level learners or what the Common European Framework (CEF) (Council of Europe, 2001) has labeled independent users.

Section 1 looks at general characteristics of this learner group. In Section 2, we will look at **syllabus** design issues in teaching reading. In Section 3, we will examine principles that can guide the teaching of reading to intermediate level readers. This will be followed in Section 4 with an examination of appropriate tasks and materials for intermediate level learners. Section 5 will allow us to address issues of teaching reading inside and outside of the classroom. The role of assessment with readers who are at the intermediate level of language proficiency is addressed in Section 6.

An intermediate level reader is defined by the Common European Framework (CEF) descriptors as someone who can:

- understand texts that consist mainly of high frequency everyday or job-related language.
- understand the description of events, feelings, and wishes in personal letters.
- read straightforward factual texts on subjects related to his field and interest with a satisfactory level of comprehension.
- scan longer texts in order to locate desired information in everyday material, such as letters, brochures, and short official documents.
- find and understand relevant information in everyday material, such as letters, brochures, and short official documents.
- identify the main conclusions in clearly signaled argumentative texts.
- recognize the line of argument in the treatment of the issue presented, but not necessarily in detail.
- recognize significant points in straightforward newspaper articles on familiar subjects.
- understand clearly written, straightforward instructions for a piece of equipment.
- read articles and reports concerned with contemporary problems in which the writers adopt particular attitudes or viewpoints.
- understand contemporary literary prose.
- read with a large degree of independence, adapting style and speed of reading to different texts and purposes, and using appropriate reference sources selectively, has broad active reading vocabulary, but may experience some difficulty with low-frequency idioms.
- scan quickly through long and complex texts, locating relevant details.

- understand in detail a wide range of lengthy, complex texts likely to be encountered in social, professional, or academic life; identifying finer points of detail including attitudes and implied as well as stated opinions.
- understand specialized articles outside her/his field, provided she/he can use a dictionary occasionally to confirm her/his interpretation of terminology.

Action

Compare the CEF descriptors for a beginning level reader (page 20) and those above for an intermediate level reader. What differences do you see between readers at the beginning level of reading proficiency and those who are at an intermediate level? Look in particular at the differences in the types of texts read as well as the reading strategies that are used.

Differences

1. _____

2. _____

3. _____

4. _____

5. _____

How would you describe to a layperson the differences between these two levels of readers?

Share your answers with a classmate or colleague. Then compare your list above with the information presented below.

As we compare the growth in **reading skills** that occurs between beginning level readers and readers at the intermediate level, we can see the progress that takes place. Table 1 outlines this growth.

	Beginning level readers	**Intermediate level readers**
Text types	postcards; simple, personal letters; short, simple texts; signs and notices; directions; informative texts	personal letters; newspapers, reports and articles; contemporary prose; instructions
Reading skills	identification of vocabulary and phrases	identification of main ideas, separation of main ideas from details, use of a dictionary, scanning, identification of conclusions

Table 1: Development in reading from beginning to intermediate levels

As readers move from the beginning level of proficiency to intermediate level, we see the growth that takes place in terms of the type of material that is read as well as the skills that are used.

2. Syllabus design issues

The intermediate level of language proficiency is a challenging level for teaching reading. The challenge for teachers is helping the readers move beyond learning to read to reading to learn. We can view this challenge visually on what I call the learning/reading continuum. Figure 1 shows the continuum.

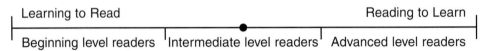

Figure 1: The learning/reading continuum

There are two things to notice about the learning/reading continuum. First, notice the placement of the dot along the continuum. It is in the middle of the continuum. When working with readers at the intermediate level of language proficiency, we should design a reading syllabus that targets opportunities to engage them in meaningful reading that will move the reader from learning to read to initial opportunities for reading to learn. At the beginning levels of language proficiency, the dot would be placed further to the left of center.

A second thing to notice about the learning/reading continuum is that it is subdivided into three levels of language proficiency. Beginning level readers are engaged in more tasks that focus on learning to read in English (i.e., the things that we dealt with in Chapter 2). At the intermediate level, we want to bridge learning to read and reading to learn. In Chapter 4, we will address things that can be done with advanced level readers to move them to the right of the continuum.

Action

What five specific things do you think that teachers can do to assist learners at the intermediate level of language proficiency to move into and through the middle of the reading continuum? (Note: we will return to your response to this question in a later activity in this chapter.)

1. _____

2. _____

3. _____

4. _____

5. _____

Share your answer with a classmate or colleague.

At the intermediate level of reading, learners should be able to read level-appropriate texts comfortably. They begin to develop a level of confidence in their reading. But there can be the danger of the learners thinking that they are better than they actually are. We call this the "**intermediate level slump**."

Jeanne Chall, a first-language reading specialist, first identified what she called the fourth grade slump for children in the United States (Chall, 1967). The basic skills of reading are being mastered, but the reader now is in a position of moving beyond the learning to read stage to learning how to get new information from texts and thus reading to learn. We see this transition from learning to read to reading to learn in the CEF descriptors that we reviewed in Section 1 of this chapter.

Reflection

If you are currently teaching, have you noticed an "intermediate level slump" in the readers that you work with? What characteristics do you notice with learners at this level?

If you are teaching now or soon will be teaching, what are some strategies you can use to help learners in the "intermediate level slump" keep making progress?

Share your ideas with a classmate or colleague.

Five syllabus design issues can help us move readers through the "intermediate level slump:" (1) keep the students reading, (2) provide interesting reading material, (3) consolidate learning before moving on, (4) integrate vocabulary instruction with reading instruction, and (5) blend intensive and extensive reading.

The first syllabus design issue is to identify ways to keep the students reading. At this level of language proficiency, the teacher plays a crucial role in encouraging students to keep reading. Recall the discussion from Chapter 1 on establishing a culture of reading. The intermediate level of language proficiency is perhaps the most vital point in the development of reading skills to establish that culture. Our instructional goal should be to have the students meaningfully engaged in reading because they want to.

Action

List three things that you could do to encourage learners to keep reading.

1. _____

2. _____

3. _____

Share your ideas with a classmate or colleague.

In my role as a reading teacher, I have consistently used the following three techniques to encourage my students to keep reading. First, I model conversations that readers have with each other. For example, in the minutes before class begins and I am waiting for students to arrive, I comment to a student on something that I recently read. I will say things like, "I was reading *Time* magazine the other day, and the article on space exploration made me think about you. Did you see that article? I'm finished reading the magazine. I can bring it tomorrow and give it to you if you would like to read it." Notice that part of this conversation results in the sharing of a magazine. The conversation is not just about what you are reading but being willing to "recycle" magazines that you are reading with your students.

The second technique is to regularly ask in class, "What are you currently reading for pleasure?" This question brings a variety of answers. Many students say they are not reading for pleasure. We talk about why they are not engaging in this exciting adventure. Sometimes it is the shyest student in the class that raises her hand and shares a title of a book she is reading. This short conversation can be an opportunity for what I call a book advertisement. Students share what they like about the book and whether they would recommend that their classmates read the book.

The final technique is to tie what we are learning in class to interests that students have. If I can find ways to explicitly link student interests to things we are reading in class, students may want to explore more reading on the topic outside of the class.

It's the little things we can say and do as a teacher that can encourage our students to keep reading.

Compare your list from the Action box on page 60 with the three suggestions I made here. What similarities and differences are there between your list and mine?

Similarities

1. _____

2. _____

Differences

1. _____

2. _____

The second syllabus design issue for teachers to keep in mind for readers at the intermediate level of language proficiency is to provide interesting reading material. We discussed this issue in Chapter 2 for working with beginning level readers. The issue is even more important at the intermediate level.

The material should allow readers to develop their reading skills. Readers are now at a stage where it is vital that they have interesting material to read. If we are going to keep the students reading, then what the students are reading must be interesting and stimulating.

The reading syllabus should include material that is not too challenging but will allow readers to use their developing reading skills to learn new things. Students need to see that they are learning new things that are interesting and important to them. Teach the students what they can do with their new level of reading ability.

Example 1 on the following page shows the table of contents from two recently published intermediate level reading textbooks. As we saw in Chapter 2, notice how the selection of thematically organized readings is used in these books.

Example 1

World Class Readings 2	*Read On 3*
Unit 1: It's a New World Record	**Chapter 1:** Dog Talk
Unit 2: Meet Koko	**Chapter 2:** It's a Dog's Life
Unit 3: The First Modern Olympic Games	**Chapter 3:** Class Afloat
Unit 4: Business Manners Around the World	**Chapter 4:** Good Manners
Unit 5: The World's Most Popular Monster	**Chapter 5:** Luv Lines
Unit 6: A Brief History of Coffee	**Chapter 6:** Zero Gravity
Unit 7: The Amazing Mr. Tesla	**Chapter 7:** Bike in a Bag
Unit 8: The ABCs of Hangul	**Chapter 8:** Around the World on Two Wheels
Unit 9: Doctors Without Borders	**Chapter 9:** Exercise for Babies
Unit 10: Sister Act: Venus and Serena Williams	**Chapter 10:** Skateboard Mom
Unit 11: Hurray for Bollywood	**Chapter 11:** Sleep Like a Baby
Unit 12: Krakatoa, West of Java	**Chapter 12:** My Dog Saved My Life
Unit 13: Examination Hell	**Chapter 13:** I Love My Job
Unit 14: The Mummy's Case	**Chapter 14:** Mexican Popsicles
	Chapter 15: The Shoe Shine Man
	Chapter 16: The Taxi Driver
	Chapter 17: Life Rolls On
	Chapter 18: The Seven-Day Race
	Chapter 19: Student Teachers
	Chapter 20: English Village
(Rogers, 2004, pages iii–iv)	(Mare, 2006, pages iv–v)

Action

With a classmate or colleague, compare the two tables of contents in Example 1. Then discuss the following questions.

1. What similarities and differences do you see in the themes?
2. What factors would influence whether these themes would be of interest to intermediate level readers? Rank the units in order of interest to intermediate level readers.
3. Do you think that the topics listed above from these two textbooks would be interesting enough to hold the attention of intermediate level readers you have worked with? Why or why not? Brainstorm a chapter list of high-interest topics for these readers.

The third syllabus design issue is to provide opportunities for readers to review what they have learned by pausing to consolidate their learning before moving on. Many textbooks build in a review opportunity, but some do not. That does not mean that the teacher must strictly follow the textbook. You can create your own review opportunities.

For example, I have taught from many reading textbooks that did not have review units. I have also found that some books have more units that I am able to cover in the time I will be with the class. There are two things that I do in this case. First, as one of the early homework assignments, I have the students review the table of contents of the book we are using. I ask them to identify the six topics of the units that they are most interested in covering. I then use the input from the students to choose which units I will cover and which ones I will not cover. Second, I organize my syllabus so that I have time to review with the students the key **reading skills** and vocabulary that they have been learning.

Some teachers have criticized this technique. They are critical that I am not using all of the textbook. They tell me that if students buy a book, they expect to use all of it and not skip parts. If this is an issue for learners you work with, you may wish to design optional out-of-class assignments for the units that are not covered in class. This keeps the class focused on high-interest topics while allowing students to make use of the whole book.

However, I emphasize that I'm teaching readers, not a book. I want to make sure that students are able to read well using the skills that I have taught them instead of hoping that by covering every unit in a book that they will become better readers.

The fourth syllabus design issue that teachers should consider is integration of vocabulary instruction and reading instruction. The "intermediate level slump" can in part be attributed to a lack of vocabulary development. The challenge for teachers is to assure that vocabulary growth continues. In terms of syllabus design issues, vocabulary instruction must be seamlessly integrated with and tied directly to reading instruction. Many appropriate reading strategies can be directly related to learning new vocabulary.

For example, you will want to teach your students how to appropriately use a dictionary. Many of our students use an electronic dictionary. Electronic dictionaries have the advantage of being easy to carry and use. But I remind my readers that when they use an electronic dictionary, there will be limits to the definitions of the words provided. Building the skill of dictionary use into classroom instruction is an important instructional objective. We will discuss this suggestion in more depth later in this chapter.

The final syllabus design issue that is important for teachers to be aware of is blending both intensive and extensive reading. If we are to make progress in helping readers move through the "intermediate slump," we have to engage them in appropriate instruction in the classroom (the explicit teaching of intensive reading skills) and provide opportunities for them to practice what they are learning with longer texts (extensive reading). We will address this issue in more depth in Section 3 of this chapter.

In Section 4 (page 71), we will examine how these suggestions for syllabus design are incorporated into actual activities for teaching intermediate level readers. We will also see examples of the basic principles that can guide the teaching of reading to intermediate learners that follow now in Section 3.

3. Principles for teaching reading to intermediate learners

Five principles can guide our teaching of reading to intermediate level learners. The five principles are:

1. focus intensively on reading strategies.
2. encourage effective use of the dictionary.
3. move readers to increase their reading rate.
4. engage in vocabulary study through learning word families.
5. provide continued focus on both intensive and extensive reading instruction.

Let's consider each of these principles and how they can help direct our efforts in the teaching of reading to intermediate level learners.

1. Focus intensely on reading strategies.

I mentioned in Chapter 2 that explicitly teaching reading strategies is a guiding principle for teaching beginning level learners. For intermediate level learners, teachers should intensify the focus on teaching reading strategies. Recall the "intermediate level slump" referred to earlier. One way of helping learners move beyond the slump is to have them effectively use reading strategies. The rationale for a more intense focus on reading strategy instruction at this level is that we want to help readers move from using strategies during in-class reading to using the strategies outside of class.

One way to intensify the teaching of the strategies is to go beyond the simple introduction of the strategy. We should help readers not only understand *how* to use the strategy but understand *why it is used* and *how to evaluate* success in the use of the strategy.

For example, when teaching the common reading strategy of skimming, it is important to move beyond the simple skimming exercises that are included in many textbooks. Take the opportunity to explain to the learners not only *what* skimming is, but *why* the strategy should be used, *how to use* the strategy, and *how to evaluate* the effective use of the strategy. Table 2 provides a framework for focusing intensely on reading strategies.

Strategy	What it is	Why we use it	How to use it	How to evaluate it
Skimming	To read something very quickly to get a general idea	To get a general idea of a reading passage so that when you read the text a second time in more depth, you are able to understand more detail	Read the first paragraph, the first sentence of other paragraphs, and the final paragraph. Look at any headings. Look at vocabulary words in italics or bold type face.	Could you tell someone else what the general idea of the reading passage is? If so, you have successfully used the strategy.

Table 2: Framework for explicit focus on reading strategies

After in-class practice of the strategy, provide opportunities for the learners to practice and use the strategy outside of class. Ask them to begin recognizing when they could use the strategy on their own. Ask learners to report in class on how they are using the strategy outside of class.

2. Encourage effective use of the dictionary.

Effective use of the dictionary is an essential skill for intermediate level readers. Many students have access to electronic dictionaries. Many use small bilingual dictionaries. Still others want to access monolingual English dictionaries. As a teacher, you should determine which type of dictionary your students use most frequently and teach them a few principles that will help them make better use of what they have.

It is also important to realize that at this point in the study of English and in the development of reading skills, readers are curious about new words that they encounter and want to get to the meaning of the word. Readers begin to notice that the multiple meanings of words can make a big difference in their reading comprehension.

The challenge for teachers is to help readers understand when to use the dictionary. The challenge I have faced as a teacher is that when I give a lesson on effective use of the dictionary, I seem to validate the use of the dictionary. Instead of helping readers know when to use it, I seem to strengthen their need to use it.

Learners can be encouraged to use the following strategies prior to resorting to a dictionary. First, readers should determine whether they have access to textual clues (i.e., dashes, colons, adjective clauses with *who* or *that*, key phrases such as *in other words* or *that is*) that will give the definition of the word. Second, they should determine if the unknown word is part of the main idea, a supporting idea, or a detail. If the word is part of the main idea, it will be very important to make sure that they understand the meaning. Finally, readers should ask themselves how many times the new word occurs in the passage. If it appears many times with no contextual hint of the meaning and the word is used in a main idea, then resorting to the use of a dictionary is appropriate. Often readers with a dependence on the dictionary will refer to the dictionary prior to using these textual clues. If these clues are not present, use of the dictionary may be appropriate.

The dictionary is a powerful tool for readers. Unfortunately, we are all familiar with learners who have an over-reliance on it. Teaching the ideas above may help intermediate level readers better understand how to use the dictionary effectively.

3. Motivate readers to increase their reading rate.

I define **reading fluency** as reading at an appropriate rate with adequate comprehension. Note that I specifically use the word *rate* and not *speed.* I do not want teachers or readers to think about speed reading (reading thousands of words per minute), but rather about reading fluently. Figure 2 illustrates this concept.

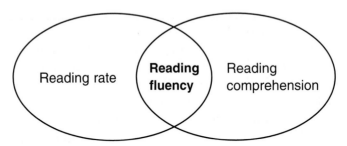

Figure 2: Reading fluency

Perhaps you are now asking yourself, *what is an appropriate rate?* and *what is adequate comprehension?* We do not read everything at the same rate nor do we seek to comprehend everything we read at the same level of understanding. For example, we do not read a newspaper at the same rate as we read a magazine article. We do not read a magazine article at the same rate as we do a novel or a textbook. As we read each of these types of texts, we do not seek 100 percent comprehension.

Grabe (1991) states that "fluent reading is rapid; the reader needs to maintain the flow of information at a sufficient rate to make connections and inferences vital to comprehension" (p. 378). Conflicting data exists regarding the optimal or sufficient reading rate. Some authorities suggest that 180 words per minute (wpm) "may be a threshold between immature and mature reading, that a speed below this is too slow for efficient comprehension or for the enjoyment of text" (Higgins and Wallace, 1989, p. 392). Dubin and Bycina (1991) state that "a rate of 200 wpm would appear to be the absolute minimum in order to read with full comprehension" (p. 181). Jensen (1986) recommends that second language readers seek to "approximate native speaker reading rates and comprehension levels in order to keep up with classmates" (p. 106). She suggests that 300 wpm is the optimal rate. This rate is supported by Nuttal (1996) and Grabe (2002).

Having worked on building students' reading rate for over 25 years, I use 200 wpm with 70 percent comprehension as the goal. This is an appropriate rate and comprehension level for readers at both the intermediate and advanced levels. The key to success is the choice of level-appropriate reading material.

Notice that this research on reading rate discusses *rate* without discussing *comprehension*. I think it is essential to discuss the development of both rate *and* comprehension. If we can get intermediate level readers to read at 200 wpm with 70 percent comprehension, they will be prepared to move out of the intermediate level slump and on to being proficient readers of English.

Do you recall the $i - 1$ discussion from Chapter 2 (pages 25–27)? I encourage teachers to use this principle when the development of reading fluency is the instructional goal. When the reading material is just a bit below their actual reading level, the learners can move through the text at a faster rate with adequate comprehension.

4. Engage in vocabulary study through learning word families.

One effective principle for improving the vocabulary skills of intermediate level readers is teaching them how to use **word families**. The focus on word families helps readers to see how they can increase their vocabulary in a very simple but powerful way.

For example, let me show you how you could teach word families using the word *assess*. Figure 3 illustrates how I begin teaching word families. I place the key word in the middle of a **word web**. I then branch off from the center with the different parts of speech. Also, if appropriate, I add a category on the word web for the use of prefixes with the word.

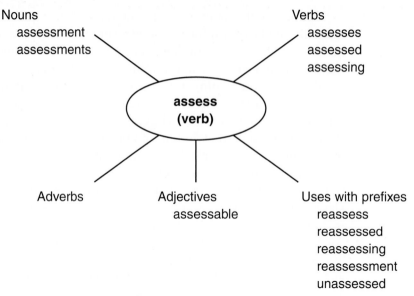

Figure 3: Word web for teaching word families

The use of this word web provides a rich opportunity to teach 12 words all in the same word family. This helps students to see how one root can be used multiple times to create other words. This also helps to raise student awareness of how learning one word can help them to learn the meanings of 11 other words.

I divide the class into small groups and assign a different word from the same word family to each of them. Their task is to identify the part of speech and the meaning of that specific word. After the groups have reported on their task, we combine the information given for the definitions to point out how similar they are and how knowing one word can help in unlocking the meaning to other words in the word family.

Create a word web that could be used for teaching word families for the vocabulary word *identify*. After creating your word web, compare it with the one I created. Mine can be found on page 88 at the end of this chapter.

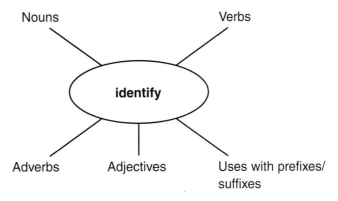

Also, by teaching word families, the teacher has another opportunity to teach how to effectively use the dictionary. At this point, it is appropriate to teach the students that all of these words might not appear in an electronic dictionary or in a small bilingual dictionary. For this activity, I encourage the use of a monolingual English dictionary. I have my students look up a word in the dictionary and then determine if there are other members of the same word family near the key word entry.

A very simple example is with the word *intense*. *Intense* is an adjective. *Intensifier* is a noun member of the family, *intensify* is a verb member of the family, and *intensely* is an adverb member of the family. When readers see the connections among these words, they can add two to three new words to their vocabulary when learning one new word.

One more thing that is helpful to teach when using these word webs for teaching word families: I focus students' attention on the correct pronunciation and word stress of each word. This adds a dimension to the learning of the words that students are very interested in.

5. Provide continued focus on both intensive and extensive reading instruction.

Recall the discussion in Chapter 1 about intensive and extensive reading (pages 8–10). **Intensive reading** instruction occurs in class and usually consists of a short reading passage followed by practice on a specific reading skill as well as comprehension and vocabulary development. **Extensive reading** involves reading increased amounts of text outside of class. One goal for effective reading instruction is to provide intensive instruction on a particular reading strategy and then provide opportunities to use the strategy outside of class during extensive reading.

At the intermediate level of instruction, we should increase the number of pages that we want students to read outside of class. To calculate the number of pages that students should be reading outside of class during extensive reading, use their projected reading fluency. If we have a goal to get students reading 200 words per minute, we could then calculate how many pages need to be read in 30 minutes at this rate. The expectation would then be to encourage students to read fluently for 30 minutes. In this way, we help build fluency at the same time that we continue to focus on both intensive and extensive reading.

Reflection

Review the five principles for teaching beginning level readers from Chapter 2 (below) and compare them with the five principles for developing intermediate level readers. Then answer the questions.

1. How do the two sets of principles compare with each other?
2. How do the principles from this chapter build on the principles from Chapter 2?
3. How do the principles for teaching intermediate level readers contribute to moving readers through the intermediate level slump and further along the learning/reading continuum?

Principles for teaching reading to beginning learners	Principles for teaching reading to intermediate learners
1. Select appropriate reading materials.	1. Focus on reading strategies.
2. Balance bottom-up, top-down, and interactive reading instruction.	2. Teach effective use of the dictionary.
3. Explicitly teach reading strategies.	3. Move students to increase their reading rate.
4. Focus attention on vocabulary development skills.	4. Improve vocabulary skills through word families.
5. Provide both intensive and extensive reading instruction.	5. Focus on both intensive and extensive reading instruction.

Summary

These five principles can guide the teaching of reading to intermediate level learners.

1. Focus intensively on reading strategies.
2. Practice effective use of the dictionary.
3. Move students to increase their reading rate.
4. Improve vocabulary skills through studying word families.
5. Continue to focus on both intensive and extensive reading instruction.

Regardless of the textbook you are using, you can incorporate these principles into your teaching. These are things that you can focus on that can help you provide effective instruction to meet the needs of your learners and help them to move through the intermediate level slump to the advanced level.

4. Tasks and materials

In this section, I will provide examples that demonstrate a range of tasks and activities that you can use to teach reading to intermediate level readers. The examples that are provided are not intended to represent all possible activity types, but rather are intended to give you ideas that you can use in your own classrooms. Based on the syllabus design issues addressed in Section 2 and the five principles for teaching intermediate level readers addressed in Section 3, we will examine four categories of useful tasks for intermediate readers.

1. Review opportunities
2. Vocabulary instruction
3. Explicit strategy instruction
4. Building reading fluency

1. Review opportunities

We reviewed the table of contents for *Read On 3* on page 62. *Read On 3* is a good example of a reading text that builds in the review opportunities. After every two chapters there is what Mare, the author, calls an Activity Menu. Example 2 shows the Activity Menu that follows Chapters 1 and 2.

Example 2

Activity Menu **CHAPTERS 1 AND 2**

1. **Tie It Together.** Think about the stories in Chapters 1 and 2. Read each sentence. Put a check in the correct column.

	DOG TALK	IT'S A DOG'S LIFE
1. Dogs can learn new words.	✔	
2. Dogs can eat at restaurants.		
3. Dogs can have a vacation.		
4. Dogs have emotions.		
5. Dogs can understand people.		
6. Dogs can take a bath in hot springs.		
7. Dogs and people can dress in the same clothes.		
8. Dogs can remember new words after one month.		

2. **Write It Down.** Choose one of the sentences from Activity 1 and write it here. Then write two sentences with more information about it.

Example: **Dogs can eat at restaurants.** The Komazawa Restaurant is in Tokyo, Japan. People and dogs can go there together to eat.

_____

_____

_____

3. **Think It Over.** What interesting information did you learn about dogs in Chapters 1 and 2? Write your answers in the chart and share them with your classmates.

STORY	INTERESTING INFORMATION
Dog Talk	
It's a Dog's Life	

4. **Just for Fun.** Use the clues in the box to complete the puzzle.

```
        2 F E T 3 C H
```

Clues

Across

2. ~~Dogs play this game with people~~

5. a place to eat.

7. what you wear

9. A microphone does this.

10. a kind of dog

Down

1. where you can buy cake

3. the people who are eating at a restaurant

4. not expensive

6. feelings

8. A dog wears this around its neck.

5. **Go Online.** Use an Internet search engine like Google. Find a clothing store for dogs where you live.

Write the Web site here. _____

What kinds of clothing do they sell? _____

Read On 3 (Mare, 2006, pages 10–11)

Reflection

How do you think that the review opportunity given above can help strengthen intermediate level readers, and perhaps more importantly, move them through the intermediate level slump?

Compare your answers with a classmate or colleague. Then look at my own ideas below. How similar are they to your answers?

I find this example of a review opportunity particularly strong. First, notice how it is not just an opportunity for students to compare answers, but to actually use knowledge that they have gained from reading the first two chapters in *Read On 3*. Second, there is a recycling of vocabulary. There is an opportunity to think about what was learned and synthesize the concepts presented in two separate chapters. Finally, there is an opportunity to have fun!

2. Vocabulary instruction

Example 3 provides explicit instruction in vocabulary development by teaching word families. Notice how there are x's placed in the table to let learners know that there is no member of that word family for the target word.

3 Focus on Vocabulary

1 Complete the chart below by adding different forms of each word. Use a dictionary to look up any words that you don't know. An **X** indicates there is no form in that category.

Noun	Verb	Adjective	Adverb
1.	accomplish		X
2. escape			X
3.	X	controversial	
4. benefit			
5.			obsessively
6.		intense	
7. perfection			
8.		practiced	X

NorthStar Intermediate, Reading and Writing, 2nd edition (Barton & Dupaquier Sardinas, 2004, page 28)

Notice the different format in this exercise for teaching word families from the word web approach that we saw earlier in this chapter. Return to the word web activity that you created on page 69. Restructure the activity in the format used in *NorthStar Intermediate, Reading and Writing* as illustrated in Example 3.

Create an additional word family exercise. Choose a word that you think intermediate level readers should learn; one that is part of a larger word family. Design an activity to teach the word family.

Did you choose to use the word web format or the chart format? Why? Explain your reason to a classmate or colleague.

3. Explicit strategy instruction

We reviewed the table of contents for *World Class Readings 2* on page 62. As you can see in Example 4, this text provides a good example of explicitly teaching reading strategies.

Example 4

Reading Skill: Skimming

Skimming is reading quickly to find the main idea. You can skim an article, a Web page, a newspaper, a textbook chapter, or a whole book. Why should you use this method? You skim if you are in a hurry, have a lot to read, or need to review something you read previously. You also skim to judge if certain material is worth reading.

Here's one basic method of skimming: First, read the first and last paragraphs, or introduction and conclusion. Next, read the first and last sentence of each paragraph. Finally, look for key words and read those parts.

Above all, read quickly: about three to four times your normal speed. Don't try to comprehend more than about 50% of the material. Don't try to understand details, and do not let unfamiliar vocabulary slow you down.

Exercise: Skim the passage below in four minutes. Then answer the questions that follow. Chart your time.

World Class Readings 2 (Rogers, 2004, page 48)

Complete the following table with information from the text in Example 4 from *World Class Readings 2*.

What is the strategy?	Why should the strategy be used?	How is the strategy used?	How can you evaluate the effective use of the strategy?

Compare your answers with the answers on page 87 at the end of this chapter. Note that in Example 4 no information is given on how to effectively evaluate the use of the strategy.

Reflection

What information could you give a group of readers that could help them determine the effective use of the reading strategy of skimming?

Compare your ideas with a classmate or colleague.

4. Building reading fluency

One frustration that I have faced as a teacher is not knowing exactly what to do to help readers increase their reading fluency. It just does not seem appropriate for me as a teacher to tell readers to "read as fast as you can." I am interested in learning some explicit activities that I can use in class to help improve reading fluency. Another challenge is that most reading textbooks for second language readers completely ignore the issue of reading fluency. I could not find any explicit activities that focus on teaching reading fluency in any textbook, except one.

I authored *ACTIVE Skills for Reading*, 2nd edition, with a clear purpose of providing teachers with some explicit activities that they can use in the classroom to build reading fluency. In the *Teacher's Manual* for the series, four in-class activities are provided that you can use to meaningfully engage readers in building their reading fluency. Look at Example 5 for the instructions for two of the activities: Rate Buildup and Repeated Reading.

Example 5

1. Rate Build-up Drill

Students are given sixty seconds to read as much material as they can. After the first sixty-second period ends, they start reading again from the beginning of the text for an additional sixty seconds. This drill is repeated a third and a fourth time. Students should be able to reread the "old" material faster and faster, extending into new material. By the end of the activity, students should be reading more material in the last sixty-second period than in the first. As students repeat this rate-building activity, their reading rate should increase. After four sixty-second periods, encourage students to continue reading the passage through to the end.

2. Repeated Reading

Students read a short passage over and over until they achieve criterion levels of reading rate and comprehension. For example, they may try to read a short 75-word paragraph three times in two minutes. The criterion levels may vary from class to class, but reasonable goals to work toward are criterion levels of 100 words per minute at 70% comprehension. After conducting this repeated reading activity, ask students to read the entire passage and then do the exercises.

ACTIVE Skills for Reading, 2nd edition, Teacher's Manual, Book 2 (Anderson, 2007, pp. 10–11)

Practice one of the activities in Example 5 on page 77. If possible, teach the activity to a group of intermediate level readers. If you do not have access to a class, practice teaching the activity to a classmate or colleague.

Action

5. Reading inside and outside of the classroom

Inside the classroom, reading instruction should focus on the explicit development of reading and comprehension skills of intermediate level readers. Outside of the classroom, there should be opportunities for readers to practice what they have learned in class. The challenge that I present to you here is to determine how you could strengthen reading inside and outside of the classroom by making explicit connections between the two types of reading.

Perhaps the greatest challenge that teachers face as they try to encourage reading both inside and outside of the classroom is, *where do I begin?* Day and Bamford (1998) and Bamford and Day (2004) provide two excellent resources for teachers who want to learn more about extensive reading. In *Extensive Reading in the Second Language Classroom*, one chapter is dedicated to setting up an extensive reading program. In this chapter, Day and Bamford ask five important questions: (1) How much material should students read? (2) How can teachers evaluate students? (3) Should students read in class or for homework or both? (4) At what level of difficulty should students read? and (5) Should students use dictionaries while reading?

The responses to these questions provide valuable insights for teachers who are seeking to encourage students to improve their reading, particularly by reading outside of the classroom. In response to the first question, *how much material should students read?*, the authors emphasize that there is no magic number of pages that determines extensive reading. "Students should read as much as is reasonably possible" (Day & Bamford, 1998, p. 84) is the primary response to this question. Teachers should consider how much time students have to complete homework for reading. Remember that part of the goal for extensive reading is to assist readers in becoming fluent readers.

Evaluation of extensive reading is a sensitive topic. Some teachers believe that reading outside the classroom should not be graded because they want students to read for the simple joy of reading and have no accountability. One alternative to no evaluation is to grade certain tasks on completion of the reading and not on the quality or correctness of the materials. Reading notebooks, weekly reading diaries, and book reports are three suggestions given by Day and Bamford. They also propose that negotiated evaluation can be an effective tool for evaluation without the high-stakes nature of tests. With negotiated evaluation, students play a role in choosing how they will be evaluated. Student input in the evaluation process makes assessment easier and fairer.

Should students read in class or for homework or both? You can probably guess the answer to this question. Reading both inside and outside of the classroom is valuable. The value of allowing time inside of the classroom for reading is to show students the value of reading. There is not enough class time to do all the reading that students should do in class. Therefore, reading outside of the classroom is necessary.

The level of difficulty of the reading material has been discussed in Chapter 2. For most extensive reading books, the student's reading goal should be reading fluency. In order to target fluency, student should choose easy books. If students are looking for books that are just below their level of language proficiency (i–1 in Krashen's input hypothesis) the material should be easy enough for successful reading.

Finally, what role do dictionaries play while reading? As previously discussed in this chapter (page 66), understanding new vocabulary through context clues is a reading strategy critical for reading success at the intermediate level. Students should be encouraged to practice this strategy during extensive reading and to read without the use of a dictionary. If a dictionary is needed, perhaps the student is reading a book that is too difficult. Teachers should remember that explicit instruction on how to appropriately use a dictionary is a valuable lesson in the reading classroom.

Day and Bamford (1998) help increase our understanding of the importance of extensive reading. The answers to these five important questions can serve as guidelines for teachers who are just beginning to take steps to include extensive reading.

Example 6 on pages 80–81 provides one specific activity from Bamford and Day that you could consider using to help you get started with extensive reading in your class. The activity is suggested by Ken Schmidt, who at the time the activity was published was teaching at Tohoku Bunka Gakuen University in Japan.

Example 6

1.2 Reading and You Questionnaire

Students fill in a reading questionnaire for homework and discuss their answers in class.

Level: Any

Aims: To help students examine their general reading habits and attitudes, as well as their feelings about reading in the new language; to give teachers insights into students' reading preferences and their attitudes toward reading in the second or foreign language for enjoyment and learning.

Preparation: Make a copy of the Reading and You questionnaire (Box 1.2) for each student. Familiarize yourself with the questions so that you can explain them to the students.

Procedure:

1. In class, distribute the questionnaire and go over any questions that might be difficult. Give examples of possible answers. Assure students that there are no right or wrong answers. Ask students to answer the questions for homework.

2. During the next class, have students work in small groups and share their answers. Tell students they may discuss whatever items seem interesting, in no particular order, for about 15 minutes.

3. Then bring the class together and ask individuals or groups to share their responses to particular questions.

4. Collect the questionnaires for later evaluation.

Contributed by: Ken Schmidt, Tohoku Bunka Gakuen University, Japan

Ken writes: "I like to use this activity just before introducing the extensive reading program. It lets us start where the students are, not with my expectations or goals. I get a chance to see how they feel about reading, and many of them, on reflection, find that they have had some pretty good experiences in the past, but may not have been doing much reading recently. It sets up a nice context in which to introduce the program. I can also adjust my introduction a bit to address some of the concerns that came up during the group discussion."

BOX 1.2 Reading and You

Name: _____   Date: __ / __ / __

1. How much time do you think you spend reading in an average week?_____ hours

2. What kinds of things (for example, novels, magazines, TV guides) do you usually read?

3. What is your favorite . . .

   magazine?   Why? (Example: "It has great photography.")

   newspaper?   Why? (Example: "I like its international news coverage.")

   book?   Why? (Example: "I really identified with the main character. It touched me.")

4. Who is your favorite writer?   Why? (Example: "Her books are so funny.")

5. Do you enjoy reading?   Why or why not? (Example: "It's boring and I don't have time" or "Reading expands my world and gives me experiences and knowledge I couldn't have gotten otherwise.")

6. What is the most interesting thing you have read about recently? (Example: "I'm reading a book now about how our memory works" or "I just read about a man who has been married fifteen times.")

7. Do you enjoy reading in English? Why or why not?

8. What is the most interesting thing you have ever read in English? (Example: "I thought *The Diary of Anne Frank* was very interesting. It helped me understand that suffering happens to real people, like me – not only to faceless people in faraway lands.")

9. If you could easily read anything in English, what would you like to read? Why? (Example: "I'd like to read *Breakfast at Tiffany's* because I liked the movie a lot.")

10. Do you think reading in English helps your English ability? If yes – how? In what way? If no – why not?

Extensive Reading Activities for Teaching Language (Schmidt, in Bamford and Day, 2004, pages 10–12)

Choose a skill from the list of reading skills below. Outline a lesson plan for explicitly teaching the skill and then identify an activity that intermediate level students could use to practice the skill during extensive reading.
Possible reading skills:

- identifying the main idea
- distinguishing between main ideas and details
- predicting
- skimming
- scanning
- understanding details
- making inferences

Share your lesson plan and activity with a classmate or colleague.

6. Assessing intermediate readers

Recall that in Chapter 2, we reviewed various types of tests. One of those was an **achievement test**. An achievement test is defined as a test used at the end of a unit or a course to see if readers learned the reading skills taught in the class. Achievement testing is an important part of any reading classroom.

Reflection

Why do you think that achievement testing is so important in a reading program?
Share your answer with a classmate or colleague.

Achievement testing is very important in all reading and language instruction programs because it is through the use of an achievement test that teachers and programs learn if they are accomplishing the program objectives. An achievement test should be developed to assess whether the specific program objectives have been achieved.

One format for an achievement test is the use of a cloze test. Cloze tests are easy to prepare and can be tied to specific objectives of vocabulary instruction as well as testing for understanding of main ideas.

A cloze test is a passage of paragraph length (typically at least four to five sentences) from which some words have been deleted. When creating a cloze test, leave the first sentence intact so the reader has sufficient context to make appropriate guesses. Usually every seventh or ninth word in a cloze activity is omitted and a blank line is put in place of the word. When **function words** like *the, a,* or *above* occur in the deletion sequence, this "rule" can be broken and delete a more appropriate word. The students' task is to read the passage with the blanks and understand it well enough to insert the missing words. One advantage of a cloze test is that you can focus on testing particular vocabulary tied to your reading program.

Cloze passages are scored either by the *exact word method* or by the *acceptable word method.* As these terms suggest, in the former, the students must insert the original word that was deleted. This procedure allows for quick and reliable scoring. In contrast, in the acceptable word method, students fill in the blanks with any word that makes sense in the passage and fits the context grammatically. Acceptable word scoring is a bit slower, but it rewards creativity and students' use of synonyms.

You can make a cloze passage out of a paragraph from your reading textbook, or you can write a new paragraph based on the topics and the vocabulary your learners have been studying. Students can either fill in the blank lines by using words they remember, or you can provide a word bank—a box above the passage with words in it. If you do give the students a word bank for assessment purposes, it is a good idea to provide more words than there are blanks in the cloze passage.

Complete the cloze passage below based on concepts that you have learned in this chapter. After completing the passage, check your answers at the end of this chapter (page 88).

In this chapter, we identified five principles to guide our teaching of reading to intermediate level learners. The five principles are first, focus _____ on reading strategies. Second, encourage effective _____ of the dictionary. Third, move readers to _____ their reading rate. Fourth, engage in _____ study through learning word families. And finally, _____ continued focus on both intensive and extensive reading instruction.

Write a 400-word passage appropriate for intermediate level readers. If you teach a class of your own, write a passage that could be used to test key vocabulary you have recently taught.

If you do not currently teach a reading class, assume that you have been teaching a unit on tourism. Use words from the following word bank in creating your reading passage.

After writing the passage, develop a cloze test of your own. Share it with a classmate or colleague.

Word Bank

tourists	first class	excited
sites	activities	transportation
famous	off the beaten path	adventure
scenery	compare	historic

7. Conclusion

In this chapter, our focus has been on teaching intermediate level readers. We identified a major challenge at the outset of the chapter, the intermediate level slump. This is the slump that readers can fall into by thinking that they are better than they really are. This slump occurs as we move from learning to read to reading to learn. Each of the six sections in this chapter helps us move readers from the intermediate level slump into advanced reading. The next chapter will focus on specific things that we can do to help readers at the advanced level.

Reflection

Let's return to an Action task from earlier in this chapter (page 59). What specific things do you think that teachers can do to assist learners at the intermediate level of language proficiency to move to the middle of the reading continuum?

_____

_____

_____

_____

_____

Compare the response you have written here to what you wrote on page 59. How has this chapter helped you learn specific things that teachers can do to move readers along the continuum?

_____

_____

_____

_____

_____

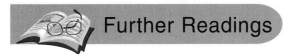

Further Readings

Burns, A. and de Silva Joyce, H. (eds.) 2000. _Teachers' Voices 5: A new look at reading practices_. Sydney, Australia: National Centre for English Language Teaching and Research, Macquarie University.

The first chapter introduces changing approaches to investigating and teaching reading. This is followed by three chapters that contain ethnographic studies discussing the reading practices of students from Lebanon, China, and El Salvador. The final three chapters address the topics of extending reading skills, appropriate texts, and integrating competencies with reading narratives.

Burns, A. and de Silva Joyce, H. (eds.) 2001. *Teachers' Voices 7: Teaching vocabulary.* Sydney, Australia: National Centre for English Language Teaching and Research, Macquarie University.

Teaching vocabulary is challenging at all levels of language proficiency. This book provides ideas for developing vocabulary with different learning groups, integrating vocabulary instruction into program curricula, vocabulary teaching techniques, and teaching idioms.

Hudson, T. 2007. Teaching Second Language Reading. New York: Oxford University Press.

Hudson supports many of the ideas presented in this chapter, including reading skills, reading strategies and metacognitive skills, and teaching issues.

Helpful Websites

TESL-EJ (http://writing.berkeley.edu/TESL-EJ/ej38/toc.html)

A quarterly Web-based journal with a wide range of teaching-related topics, reviews (of textbooks, teacher resource books, media and websites), and discussion forum.

The Reading Matrix (http://www.readingmatrix.com)

The *Reading Matrix* is an online journal for teachers and an excellent teacher resource. The focus is on teaching ESL/EFL reading. This site will provide additional ideas on ways to help you teach intermediate level readers.

The International Reading Association (www.reading.org/)

The International Reading Association is an organization for teachers and researchers interested in the teaching of reading to all age groups. Their website provides links to interesting information and publications of interest.

TESOL (www.tesol.org/)

Teachers of English to Speakers of Other Languages is a professional association dedicated to helping teachers and researchers interested in working with non-native speakers of English. Although teaching reading is not one of their primary areas of focus, some resources are available for teachers interested in reading.

References

Bamford, J. and R.R. Day. (Eds.) 2004. *Extensive Reading Activities for Teaching Language.* New York, NY: Cambridge University Press.

Chall, J.S. 1967. *Learning to Read: The great debate.* New York, NY: McGraw-Hill.

Council of Europe. 2001. *Common European Framework of Reference for Languages: Learning, Teaching, Assessment.* Cambridge, UK: Cambridge University Press.

Day, R.R. and J. Bamford. 1998. *Extensive Reading in the Second Language Classroom.* New York, NY: Cambridge University Press.

Dubin, F. and D. Bycina. 1991. Academic Reading and the ESL/EFL Teacher. In M. Celce-Murcia (Ed.), *Teaching English as a Second or Foreign Language* (2nd ed.) (pp. 195–215). New York, NY: Newbury House.

Grabe, W. 1991. Current Developments in Second Language Reading Research. *TESOL Quarterly, 25,* 375–406.

Grabe, W. 2002. Reading in a Second Language. In R.B. Kaplan (Ed.), *The Oxford Handbook of Applied Linguistics* (pp. 49–59). New York, NY: Oxford University Press.

Higgins, J. and R. Wallace. 1989. Hopalong: A computer reader pacer. *System, 17,* 389–399.

Jensen, L. 1986. Advanced Reading Skills in a Comprehensive Course. In F. Dubin, D.E. Eskey, and W. Grabe (Eds.) *Teaching Second language Reading for Academic Purposes* (pp. 103–124). Reading, MA: Addison-Wesley Publishing.

Nuttall, C. 2005. *Teaching Reading Skills in a Foreign Language,* 3rd ed. Oxford, UK: Heinemann.

Answer Key for the Action Box on page 69.

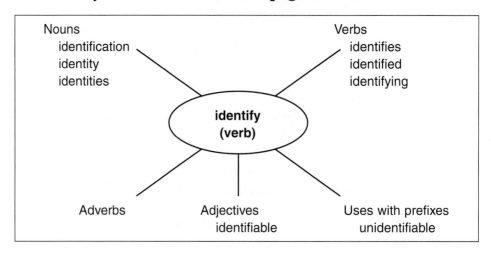

Answer from the Action Box on page 76.

What is the strategy?	Why should the strategy be used?	How is the strategy used?	How can you evaluate the effective use of the strategy?
Skimming	If you are in a hurry, have a lot to read, or need to review something you read previously. You also skim to judge if certain material is worth reading.	First, read the first and last paragraphs, or introduction and conclusion. Next, read the first and last sentence of each paragraph. Finally, look for key words and read those parts.	Not given in this information.

Answer Key for Action Box on page 83.

In this chapter, we identified five principles to guide our teaching of reading to intermediate level learners. The five principles are first, focus <u>intensely</u> on reading strategies. Second, encourage effective <u>use</u> of the dictionary. Third, move readers to <u>increase</u> their reading rate. Fourth, engage in <u>vocabulary</u> study through learning word families. And finally, <u>provide</u> continued focus on both intensive and extensive reading instruction.

Chapter **Four**

Reading for advanced level learners

At the end of this chapter, you should be able to:

Goals

 describe what makes a reader at an advanced level of language proficiency different from readers at the beginning and intermediate levels.

 identify important reading syllabus design issues.

 explain key principles to support the teaching of reading to advanced learners.

 create materials and activities for explicit teaching of reading inside and outside of the classroom to advanced learners.

 identify how to prepare vocabulary tests for advanced readers.

1. Introduction

In Chapters 2 and 3, we considered important principles for teaching reading to English language learners at the beginning and intermediate levels of language proficiency. We will continue to rely on the Common European Framework (CEF) (Council of Europe, 2001) and the descriptors for proficient users (advanced level readers) as we address syllabus design issues. This will be followed by a discussion of the principles for teaching reading to learners at an advanced level of language proficiency. Next, we will discuss reading tasks and materials for advanced learners. Then we will identify how to strengthen the teaching of reading both inside and outside of the classroom. This will be followed by a discussion of key issues that teachers should be aware of while assessing advanced readers.

The CEF descriptors define proficient users of English (advanced level readers) as people who can:

- understand any correspondence, given the occasional use of a dictionary.
- understand in detail lengthy, complex texts, whether or not they relate to their area of specialty, provided they can reread difficult sections.
- read with ease virtually all forms of the written language, including abstract, structurally, or linguistically complex texts such as manuals, specialized articles, and literary works.
- understand a wide range of long and complex texts, appreciating the subtle distinctions of style and implicit as well as explicit meaning.

1. What makes an advanced level reader different from a beginning or intermediate level reader? Compare the CEF descriptors for beginning and intermediate level readers (pages 20 and 56) and those above for advanced level readers. What differences do you see between readers at the beginning and intermediate levels of reading proficiency and those who are at an advanced level? Look in particular at the differences in the types of texts read as well as the reading strategies that are used. List five differences below.

   a. _____

   b. _____

   c. _____

   d. _____

   e. _____

2. How could you describe to someone not familiar with second language readers the differences among these three levels of readers?

3. How will you interact differently with readers with an advanced level of language proficiency from readers at the beginning and intermediate levels?

Share your answers with a classmate or colleague. Compare your lists in Question 1 with the information presented below.

As we compare the growth in reading skills that occurs among readers at beginning, intermediate, and advanced levels of language proficiency, we can see the progress that takes place. Table 1 outlines this growth.

	Beginning level readers	**Intermediate level readers**	**Advanced level readers**
Text types	postcards; simple, personal letters; short, simple texts; signs and notices; directions; informative texts	personal letters; newspapers, reports and articles; contemporary prose; instructions	long, complex texts used in academic, professional, and social contexts; complex instructions contained in manuals as well as literary and non-literary texts
Reading skills	identification of vocabulary and phrases	identification of main ideas, separation of main ideas from details, use of a dictionary, scanning, identification of conclusions	identification of abstract ideas, rereading with a specific purpose

Table 1: Development in reading from beginning to intermediate to advanced levels

As readers move from the beginning to intermediate and then to advanced levels of language proficiency, we see the growth that takes place in terms of the type of material that is read as well as the skills that are used.

2. Syllabus design issues

When working with readers at an advanced level of language proficiency, there are four **syllabus** design questions that should be kept in mind. First, what drives the syllabus: the textbook or curricular goals? Second, does the syllabus move the reader further along the learning/reading continuum? Third, does the syllabus begin to provide more authentic texts and opportunities to read academic materials? Fourth, does the syllabus provide meaningful opportunities to integrate reading with other language skills? We will consider each of these questions in detail in this section.

Let's consider the first syllabus design question for working with advanced level readers. What drives the syllabus: the textbook or curricular goals? In many language teaching contexts around the world, the syllabus is set by the textbook that is used. Teachers are expected to simply follow the chapters in sequence. In other programs, teachers or a curriculum coordinator may write curriculum goals and coordinate the development of the curriculum across skill areas and across levels of language proficiency in the program. In the latter case, the curriculum coordinator might select an appropriate text that best matches the goals for a particular level of instruction and then supplement the text with additional reading material to meet the program goals. In either case, programs may target a particular type of language learner (i.e., learners seeking to attend a university in an English-speaking country or learners who are immigrant adults and need English for non-academic purposes). I believe that it is vital for teachers to know what drives the curriculum when working with advanced level readers.

Action

What do you think should drive a reading curriculum? A textbook or curricular goals? If you were the curriculum coordinator, what learner factors (i.e., age, socio-economic status, level of proficiency) would influence the curriculum? What other factors (i.e., size of the school, funding) would also have an impact? Why?

_____

_____

_____

_____

_____

Share your answers with a classmate or colleague.

_____

A second syllabus design question that teachers should consider is whether the syllabus moves the reader further along the reading continuum. Recall our discussion in Chapter 3 (page 58) about the learning/reading continuum. Figure 1 shows the continuum.

Learning to Read   Reading to Learn

Figure 1: The learning/reading continuum

Notice the placement of the dot along the continuum. When working with readers at the advanced level, we should design a reading syllabus that targets opportunities to engage them in meaningful reading that will help them to learn new information. However, let me issue a word of caution. We should remember that we are working with individuals who are still developing their language proficiency to some extent. These readers still have some things to learn about learning to read. Thus, the dot is not completely at the far right end of the continuum.

Action

What specific things do you think teachers can do to assist learners in moving further to the right along the reading continuum? List three to five specific things that you think can be done. (Note: we will return to your response to this question in a later activity in this chapter.)

1. _____

2. _____

3. _____

4. _____

5. _____

Share your answers with a classmate or colleague.

A third syllabus design question that we should consider is whether the syllabus begins to provide more authentic texts and opportunities to read materials appropriate for the learners' goals outside of the classroom (i.e., academic reading for those going on to higher education studies in English; professional materials for learners working in an English-speaking environment). In your response above, did you mention the use of more authentic texts and opportunities to read appropriate materials as a way to move readers along the continuum? This step would certainly be one way to help learners read to learn.

Example 1 is the table of contents from two reading texts designed for readers at the advanced level. Notice the titles of the textbooks as well as the titles of the units and chapters.

Example 1

On Location 3: Reading and Writing for Success in the Content Areas	*Quest 3: Reading and Writing,* 2nd ed.
Unit 1: I'll Never Forget . . .	**Unit 1:** Anthropology
Unit 2: Loud and Ugly	**Chapter 1** Cultural Anthropology
Unit 3: Surviving Homework	**Chapter 2** Physical Anthropology
Unit 4: Ancient Worlds	**Unit 2:** Economics
Unit 5: Who's Smarter . . . Cats or Dogs?	**Chapter 3** Developing Nations
Unit 6: How to Make Really Neat Stuff	**Chapter 4** The Global Economy
Unit 7: What were the 1960s Like, Grandpa?	**Unit 3:** Literature
Unit 8: Pro or Con?	**Chapter 5** The Nature of Poetry
Unit 9: I Can't Put it Down!	**Chapter 6** Heroes in Literature
Unit 10: The Perfect Storm	**Unit 4:** Ecology
	Chapter 7 Endangered Species
	Chapter 8 Human Ecology
(Bye, 2005, pages iv–vii)	(Hartmann and Blass, 2007, page iv)

Reflection

Do you notice any differences between these two tables of contents and those we have seen in Chapters 2 (page 22) and 3 (page 62) for readers at the beginning and intermediate levels? What principles of syllabus design discussed so far do you see illustrated in the tables of contents above?

Share your answers with a classmate or colleague.

One possible response you could have given to the reflection above is that textbooks for readers at the advanced level of proficiency feature more authentic texts and academic materials with a high level of vocabulary. Notice in particular the titles of the units in *Quest 3: Reading and Writing*, 2nd ed. listed above. We will discuss academic vocabulary in the next section of this chapter as we identify specific principles that can guide our work at this level.

A final syllabus design question we will consider in this chapter is whether the syllabus provides meaningful opportunities to integrate reading with other language skills. When designing a syllabus for teaching reading to advanced level learners, we should be aware that integration of language skills will be much more important at this level than at beginning and intermediate levels. How are writing tasks meaningfully integrated into reading tasks? How are listening and speaking integrated into what is read? These are questions that we will consider in detail in Sections 3 and 4 of the chapter.

Perhaps you have noticed how the syllabus design issues all work together in strengthening a reader's ability to read to learn and to do something with what is read. At this level of reading, teachers should look for opportunities for readers to use what they are reading with other language skills.

3. Principles for teaching reading to advanced learners

In this section, we will address five principles that are particularly important for teaching reading to advanced level learners:

1. Integrate reading with other language skills by placing reading at the core of instruction.
2. Help readers improve vocabulary skills through academic vocabulary instruction.
3. Focus on academic reading strategies to help advanced readers take responsibility for their own learning.
4. Teach advanced readers how reading on the computer is different from reading print material.
5. Ensure that readers at the advanced level of language proficiency are reading fluently.

1. Integrate reading with other language skills by placing reading at the core of instruction.

In an online teacher education course on teaching reading (Anderson, 2006), I present what I consider a helpful way to integrate reading activities with other language skills. I encourage teachers to think about how they can place reading at the core of instruction. Figure 2 on page 96 provides a visual representation of this idea.

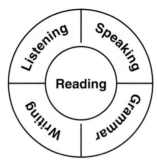

Figure 2: Placing reading at the core of instruction

When we are working with readers at the advanced level, one important principle that should guide our work is to provide meaningful opportunities for the readers to use what they are learning while reading in combination with other language skills. Once readers have new knowledge from a text, how are they writing about it? How are they speaking about it? How are they using the knowledge as they listen to information on the same topic? These are all questions that teachers should consider.

The meaningful integration of the language skills will provide a focused purpose for reading. Ediger (2006) points out that reading purpose is addressed in reading research but that "few go the next step to spell out *how* to focus reading toward accomplishing the purpose that one has set" (p. 312, italics in original). I believe that placing reading at the core of instruction and then identifying how to integrate the other language skills is one explicit way that we can focus on reading purpose. When you read knowing that you have to write a summary of what you have read, there will be a clear purpose for reading. When you read knowing that you are going to listen to an academic lecture on the same topic, you have a meaningful purpose for reading. These are all tasks that readers at the advanced level of language proficiency will have to perform.

Integrating reading with other language skills by placing reading at the core is one important reading principle that language teachers should focus on for readers at this level of proficiency. Refer back to Example 1 on page 94 which contains the tables of contents for *On Location 3: Reading and Writing for Success in the Content Areas* and *Quest 3: Reading and Writing,* 2nd ed. The titles of the textbooks include both reading and writing. This highlights what can be a natural integration of writing with reading.

2. Help readers improve vocabulary skills through academic vocabulary instruction.

The demands of vocabulary become a much more important feature of reading at the advanced levels of language proficiency. Specialized vocabulary plays an important part of reading at this level. Academic, non-academic, and professional texts all require higher-level social and work-related vocabulary.

Readers are expected to engage in higher-order thinking activities and interact with others based on what they have read.

In 1953, Richard West developed what he called the General Service List (GSL) (West, 1953). The 2,000 most frequent vocabulary words in English were identified in this list. Even though the list was developed almost 55 years ago, the frequency of common words in English has not changed significantly. Teachers can use the GSL in particular to assist learners at the beginning and intermediate levels of language proficiency. Advanced ESL/EFL readers should know these words as well.

Research suggests that to be successful in studying at an English-speaking university, learners need a vocabulary size of at least 10,000 words (Hazenberg, 1996). Many teachers are probably aware of the Academic Word List (AWL) (Coxhead, 2000). If you are not, the list is available electronically from the Simple English Wiktionary website (http://simple.wiktionary.org/wiki/Wiktionary:Academic_word_list).

In the 1980s, Zue and Nation (1984) published a list of important vocabulary necessary for academic reading. Building on this earlier success, Coxhead, at the University of Wellington, New Zealand, refined the list from a written academic **corpus**. Using texts from liberal arts, commerce, law, and science, Coxhead identified 570 **headwords** of **word families** that are high frequency words in academic contexts. These words were not part of the most frequent 2,000 words in English. Coxhead divided the 570 headwords into 10 sublists.

Two examples may be helpful to explain how the AWL works. The word *analyse* (note the British spelling) is an academic word from Coxhead's first sublist. This is a headword. There are 15 words that are part of the word family: *analysed, analyzer, analysers, analyses, analyzing, analysis, analyst, analysts, analytic, analytical, analytically, analyze, analyzed, analyzes,* and *analyzing.* I think that it is important to teach readers the variations between the British and the American spellings because they may encounter both while reading. As discussed in Chapter 3 for intermediate learners, teachers of advanced level readers should help readers to learn the headword, its spelling, and meaning. It is then easy to learn the variations that are part of the word family. I have found it particularly useful to have students identify which words in the word family are nouns, verbs, adjectives, or adverbs. In this way, students have the opportunity to add significantly to their vocabulary. The word *analyse* is one of the 570 headwords on the AWL. Knowing that word and its 15 derivations adds 16 words to our vocabulary knowledge bank.

A second example from sublist 8 may also be useful. One of the headwords on this list is *chart.* There are four words that are part of the word family for *chart: charted, charting, charts, uncharted.* Note here how the prefix *un-* is added to the headword. Students learn several useful prefixes as they study the AWL and in this way, improve their vocabulary skills through explicit academic vocabulary instruction.

3. Focus on academic reading strategies to help advanced readers take responsibility for their own learning.

One of the most frequent questions that I am asked about reading strategies is where to locate a list of appropriate strategies to consider for instruction. In example 2, Gunderson (1991) provides the following very useful list of 34 content reading strategies that are valuable to explicitly teach to advanced level readers.

Example 2

1. recognize the significance of the content
2. recognize important details
3. recognize unrelated details
4. find the main idea of a paragraph
5. find the main idea of large sections of discourse
6. differentiate fact and opinion
7. locate topic sentences
8. locate answers to specific questions
9. make inferences about content
10. critically evaluate content
11. realize an author's purpose
12. determine the accuracy of information
13. use a table of contents
14. use an index
15. use a library card catalog (note: in 1991 when this text was published, libraries did not use online catalogs. Today, more than 15 years later, an online catalog is the norm for a library.)
16. use appendices

17. read and interpret tables
18. read and interpret graphs
19. read and interpret charts
20. read and interpret maps
21. read and interpret cartoons
22. read and interpret diagrams
23. read and interpret pictures
24. read and interpret formulae
25. read and understand written problems
26. read and understand expository material
27. read and understand argument
28. read and understand descriptive material
29. read and understand categories
30. adjust reading rate relative to purpose of reading
31. adjust reading rate relative to difficulty of material
32. scan for specific information
33. skim for important ideas
34. learn new material from text

(Gunderson, 1991, pages 145–146)

It is absolutely essential that teachers realize that good readers do not use single strategies in isolation. Strategies are used in combination with other strategies. They are used in what is often referred to as strategy clusters. For example, a cluster of four strategies from the list above would be a natural combination when preparing for an academic task of writing an argumentative research paper. While reading from different sources, they will have to realize the author's purpose for writing (strategy 11), find the main idea of large sections of written text (strategy 5), then differentiate between facts and opinions (strategy 6), and then finally critically evaluate the content (strategy 10). The four strategies of this cluster naturally support each other in the task. There might be additional strategies that readers will use as well.

Action

Review the list of 34 academic reading strategies outlined in Example 2. If you are teaching, how many of these strategies do you already explicitly teach?

Select one of the strategies and identify what other strategies might be used with it in a strategy cluster. List them below.

_____

_____

_____

_____

Outline how you might go about teaching the strategy cluster to advanced level readers.

_____

_____

_____

_____

_____

Share your answers with a classmate or colleague.

_____

4. Teach advanced readers how reading on the computer is different from reading print material.

Computers and the Internet play an increasingly important role in the lives of second language (**L2**) readers around the world. Online reading serves as the source of input for thousands of L2 readers. With the increased use of computers comes the increased need to train language learners how to read online. More and more L2 classrooms are engaging learners in online learning tasks (Bikowski & Kessler, 2002; Ioannou-Georgiou, 2002; Sutherland-Smith, 2002; Warschauer, 1997, 1999, 2002). Very little research to date has reported on the similarities and differences between reading online and reading traditional print materials.

Murray (2005) points out that "there has been an assumption that the literacies of print texts will necessarily transfer to the new media without intervention" (p. viii). Based on research that Murray and a colleague conducted in Australia (Murray & McPherson, 2005) "print literacy does not necessarily transfer to digital literacy" (Murray, 2005, p. viii).

One aspect of reading that has been addressed with first language readers in the online versus print reading environments is reading speed. Kurniawan and Zaphiris (2001) report on a study in which they tested reader preferences for reading online or printed texts with one, two, or three columns. The data do not suggest that readers have a preference between online or printed texts. They also investigated reading speeds in both contexts to determine if there is a difference in the two reading contexts. Their data suggests that reading on paper was 10–30 percent faster than reading online in the one and two column formats. No differences were found in the two contexts with three column readings. Kurniawan and Zaphiris conclude that designers of online materials should be aware that reading will be slower in the online context and therefore should do all they can to enhance online reading materials.

In a study I conducted (Anderson, 2003), I report on research that addressed two research questions: (1) What are the online reading strategies used by second language readers? and (2) Do the online reading strategies of English as a second language readers (**ESL**) differ from those of English as a foreign language readers (**EFL**)?

Participants in this study consisted of 247 L2 readers. One hundred thirty-one (53 percent) of the learners were studying EFL at the Centro Cultural Costarricense Norteamericano (CCCN) in San José, Costa Rica. The remaining 116 (47 percent) were studying in an ESL environment at the English Language Center (ELC) at Brigham Young University, in Provo, Utah. The *Survey of Reading Strategies* (SORS) (Sheorey and Mokhtari, 2001) was adapted for use in this research project. The adapted Online SORS (OSORS) consists of 38 items that measure metacognitive reading strategies. The 38 items are subdivided into three categories: global reading strategies (18 items), problem solving strategies (11 items), and support strategies (9 items).

Perhaps the greatest outcome of this research is the recognition of the importance of metacognitive online reading strategies for second language learners. This strategy type plays a more important role in L2 reading instruction than perhaps we have previously considered. When classroom teachers engage their learners in online learning tasks, a strategy awareness and training component is essential. L2 reading teachers can focus learner attention on the metacognitive reading strategies identified in the OSORS to help learners improve their online reading ability. The metacognitive strategies listed in the OSORS are included with a copy of the survey in Appendices 1 and 2 beginning on page 157.

Tindale (2005) outlines various issues that teachers should take into consideration when engaging learners in reading electronic texts. She lists specific questions in four areas: breaking the code, participating in understanding texts, using texts, and analyzing texts. One key question from each of these four areas illustrates the challenges ahead of teachers in working with print and online reading. For breaking the code, Tindale asks: "What physical characteristics of electronic texts have an impact on learners' ability to read them (for example screen characteristics, text characteristics, and the use of different fonts and colours)?" In the area related to participating in understanding texts, one sample question is "What do learners need to know about navigational elements of webpages (for example navigation bars, pull-down or pop-up menus, and 'back' buttons)?" From the area of using texts, Tindale asks, "How is the structure and organization of a web text linked to the meaning and purpose of the text?" Finally, from the area of analyzing texts, one sample question is "What teaching and learning activities will help learners develop an understanding of what the web excludes as well what it includes?" (Tindale, 2005, pp. 10–11).

The important principle that teachers should remember here is that we cannot assume that readers can (or will) naturally transfer the reading strategies they use while reading print materials to reading material on the Internet. We need to think about how we will train readers about the differences between these two reading contexts.

5. Ensure that advanced level readers are reading fluently.

Professor Jay Samuels is perhaps the leading reading teacher/researcher in the world. His main interest is **reading fluency**. Since the 1970s, he has directed his attention to the topic of fluency and how to help teachers understand what they can do in the classroom to assist readers who are struggling to improve their reading fluency.

Samuels (2006) points out that reading fluency is tied to **automaticity theory**: People who are highly skilled at certain tasks are able to devote their attention to doing more than one thing. They are able to multi-task. When engaged in multi-tasking, you are able to split your attention among different tasks. Beginning level readers are using their cognitive capacity to decode the words and connect the word with its meaning. The more exposure that readers have to words, the less cognitive capacity they need to understand the word and its meaning. To be a fluent reader, one must automatically process a word and its meaning quickly without much thought.

To further explain the concept of automaticity, let me give a non-reading example. As a graduate student at the University of Texas at Austin, I often drove my car to campus. One beautiful fall afternoon, I left campus to drive home. It was late in the afternoon, about 6:00 P.M. The sky was a crystal clear blue. I listened to the radio and enjoyed the drive home. My mind wandered as I thought about the beauty of the day and about the tasks I had to complete that evening.

As I arrived home and shut off the car, I was struck with amazement. I didn't remember crossing the bridge. I didn't remember taking the exit from the freeway. I didn't remember using the turn signal, although I am confident that I must have because it was my habit to do so. At first I was a bit scared. What if every other driver on the road that afternoon had the same experience?

The next morning, I left early to teach my 8:00 A.M. ESL writing course. As I left the house it was raining. I started the car and pulled away from the house. I turned on the windshield wipers and discovered that they were broken. I proceeded slowly, hoping that I would be able to drive safely. I realized immediately that I had to turn off the radio (it was on from my drive home the previous day). I was very much aware of everything that I was doing as a driver. I was aware of the pressure of my foot on the gas and brake pedals. I was aware of giving the drivers around me plenty of time to know that I was changing lanes, so I turned on my turn signals. My full attention was on every aspect of my driving. By the time I arrived at the university, I was mentally exhausted!

On the evening before, I had driven home using automatic driving skills. My cognitive capacity was directed to other things. Driving in the rain without windshield wipers required all of my cognitive capacity. I was not able to multi-task at all. The driving conditions were so poor that I could not use my cognitive capacity for anything except driving.

This experience has always served as the reminder for me that readers who are struggling are not able to use their cognitive capacity to integrate what they are reading with what they already know. They are not able to think about how they are going to use what they are reading with other language skills. Their full attention is on decoding the words. These readers are not fluent. They cannot automatically process the words and think about other things.

The principle of building fluent readers is especially important at the advanced levels of language proficiency. In the next three sections, we will outline specific things that teachers can do to build more fluent readers.

4. Tasks and materials

The focus for this section is on providing a description and examples of appropriate tasks and materials that can be used with readers at the advanced level of language proficiency. Most of these examples illustrate the principles described in this chapter. The following four task and exercise types are explained in this section:

1. Integrated reading tasks
2. Vocabulary learning tasks

3. Reading strategies and tasks

4. Fluent reading tasks

The integration of reading with other language skills is very important at the advanced level of language proficiency. Readers should be able to make the connections between what they are reading about, listening to, speaking about, and writing about. At this level, teachers should capitalize on opportunities to have readers use what they are reading for more than reading itself.

Example 3 illustrates this principle very well. From *NorthStar Reading and Writing, Advanced*, Unit 3 is entitled *The Road to Success*.

Example 3

1 Look at the following flowchart. The outcome is a career change. Work in pairs. Discuss the personal qualities required to ease the passage from one stage to the next. Write a quality for at least four of the different stages.

become aware of job dissatisfaction → quit job

begin job search → go to career-change workshops or career counselor → get job rejections

research possible careers

interview

rewrite résumé

apply for more jobs

apply for jobs

get job offer → quit old job

start new job

Example

Stage	Quality
quit job	courage

NorthStar Reading and Writing, Advanced (Cohen and Miller, 2006, page 51)

Section 1 of the *NorthStar* unit prepares the reader for successfully engaging with the text and integrating what is read with writing, providing a flowchart as a mental map of concepts in the reading. Later in the unit, students make predictions about the reading by looking at a picture of climbers ascending a snow-covered mountain. They are asked if the photo is a good representation of the struggle for success. Readers must share their thoughts with another student. Right away, readers are speaking about the topic—the road to success—with someone else and justifying why they think the photo represents a struggle. The next preparation step asks the readers to complete a hope-scale survey by working in a small group. They ask classmates if they are pessimistic, optimistic, or in-between and why. Finally, readers take a self-discovery quiz. The quiz is designed to help readers see a connection between their outlook on life (optimism, pessimism, etc.) and their potential for success. The connection between hope and success is made and readers prepare to read about a character, Katie, in a reading entitled "Gotta Dance."

The reading, "Gotta Dance," by Jackson Jodie Daviss, is an authentic passage, not something written specifically for second language readers. The passage is 2,250 words in length. The story describes Katie's dream of becoming a dancer, even when her entire family discourages her. The text is ideal for making inferences about a brother who recently passed away before living his dream. Katie doesn't want to miss out on her dream, so she leaves her small Midwestern town and "goes on tour," dancing from city to city.

Reading comprehension (main ideas and details) is checked, followed by reactions to the reading which are shared in small groups, again allowing another opportunity to practice speaking. The unit continues with a second, shorter reading by Dennis O'Grady, "Keeping Your Confidence Up" (370 words). These two readings provide a strong foundation in reading and speaking. Vocabulary instruction follows in section 3 of the unit.

The strength of *NorthStar Reading and Writing, Advanced* is the manner in which the writing activity book builds on everything that has been completed in the main text. Students engage in a **process approach to writing**. For this unit, they write a descriptive essay about the qualities they believe are necessary to accomplish a personal dream of success. Using the texts from the reading book, writers are involved in prewriting, organizing, peer review, revising, and editing activities. The explicit connection between reading and writing and the integration of the skills is very nicely done in this level of *NorthStar*.

Reflection

What is your reaction to the way that *NorthStar Reading and Writing, Advanced* integrates listening, speaking, reading, and writing? Are you familiar with other texts that integrate the skills?

Share your answers with a classmate or colleague.

2. Vocabulary learning tasks

For readers at the advanced level, working with academic vocabulary is particularly challenging. Teachers should look for opportunities to challenge readers with vocabulary that they will encounter while reading academic textbooks. The use of the term *academic vocabulary* should not lead us to believe that this vocabulary is only used in academic contexts. This vocabulary will be found in a wide variety of professional contexts. All learners at the advanced level of proficiency, regardless of their professional or vocational pursuits, will encounter this vocabulary.

Two recent publications are a great resource for teachers working with advanced level readers who want to gain mastery of the academic word list. *Essential Academic Vocabulary: Mastering the Complete Academic Word List* (Huntley, 2006) and *Focus on Vocabulary: Mastering the Academic Word List* (Schmitt & Schmitt, 2005) provide excellent exercises for students to practice. The value of these two publications is that they organize the 10 sublists from the AWL into direct vocabulary instruction and appropriate exercises for advanced level readers.

Huntley provides vocabulary practice through preview questions, a reading, vocabulary in context practice, reading comprehension exercises, dictionary skills, word forms in sentences, collocations, word parts, writing practice, and speaking practice. Learners encounter the words in meaningful contexts and with meaningful practice.

Example 4

HISTORY

WORD LIST

Noun		Verb	Adjective	Adverb
emigration	instability	accommodate	dynamic	implicitly
enhancement	motivation	assign	ideological	ultimately
estate	network	dispose	manual	
expansion	perspective	enable	medical	
exploitation	pursuit	enforce	radical	
exposure	revolution	exceed	subordinate	
hierarchy	survival	sustain	underlying	
incentive	transformation		visible	
incidence	transition			
input	transportation			

1. What was the Industrial Revolution? Where and when did it take place?

2. Before the Industrial Revolution, what kind of work did most poor people do and where did they live? What happened to these people when the Industrial Revolution began?

3. What changes in society happened during the Industrial Revolution? How did it change the way people lived?

4. What were working conditions like at this time? Give examples of how and where men, women, and children worked.

5. What were some consequences of the Industrial Revolution for rich people and for poor people?

READING

THE IMPACT OF THE INDUSTRIAL REVOLUTION

1 Although inventions were the most **visible** and **dynamic** aspects of the Industrial **Revolution** in Europe, many other **transformations** in the **hierarchies** of society, politics, **transportation**, and the economy took place. These early changes—including smoky cities, slum neighborhoods, polluted water, child **manual** labor in mines and textile mills—transformed entire regions into
5 industrial landscapes.

The most dramatic environmental changes brought about by industrialization occurred in the **expansion** of urban areas in Europe. London, one of the largest cities in 1700 with 500,000 inhabitants, grew to 959,000 by 1800 and **exceeded** 2,363,000 by 1850, by then the largest city in the world. Smaller towns grew even faster. Manchester's population increased eightfold in a
10 century. Liverpool grew sixfold in the first 60 years of the nineteenth century.

6. WORD PARTS

trans- (across, changed)

The prefix *trans-* means "across" or "changed."

6A Match the verbs in the left column to the item that is moved or altered in the right column.

1. _____ transfer	**a.** heart
2. _____ transform	**b.** book
3. _____ translate	**c.** business
4. _____ transmit	**d.** electronic messages
5. _____ transplant	**e.** environment
6. _____ transport	**f.** grades
7. _____ transact	**g.** goods
8. _____ transfuse	**h.** blood

6A Match the verbs in the left column to the item that is moved or altered in the right column.

1. _____ transfer   a. heart
2. _____ transform   b. book
3. _____ translate   c. business
4. _____ transmit   d. electronic messages
5. _____ transplant   e. environment
6. _____ transport   f. grades
7. _____ transact   g. goods
8. _____ transfuse   h. blood

6B Make the following verbs into nouns by adding the appropriate noun suffix endings where needed.

Verb	Noun
transfuse	
transport	
transform	
transmit	
transact	
translate	
transplant	
transfer	

7. WRITING

7A Writing a Summary

See *Appendix IV* for additional infor

Reread the article "The Impact of the
Revolution on the Internet. Take note
your notes to summarize the reading.

7B Paragraph Writing

Write a response to **one** of the following topics about living in the time of the Industrial Revolution. Include at least **six to eight vocabulary words** in your paragraph.

1. You are a young married woman with three children under the age of six. You have recently moved to Manchester with your husband and children to find work in the textile factories. Describe a day in your new life, adding details about your housing situation, your job and your husband's job, the problems of childcare, and your concerns about the unhealthy environment you now have to live in. Compare this situation with your former life in a small farming village. Have you made the right decision in moving to Manchester?

2. You are a young unmarried man. You have been working in the coal mines of northern England for ten years (since you were a child of ten), and you are very dissatisfied with your present life. You have recently become involved with labor conflicts, and you are now on strike trying to enhance the working conditions for the coal miners in your region. You are considering the possibility of emigrating to the United States, where you hope you would find a better life. Write a letter to your parents in the countryside describing your working conditions and explain to them why you are thinking about emigrating.

8. SPEAKING

8A A Cooperative Learning Research Project

As a small group, choose a topic related to the Industrial Revolution to research. Topics could include the following:

- the causes of the Industrial Revolution
- child labor
- housing conditions
- population shifts
- working in a coal mine

- working in a textile mill
- health problems
- transportation
- working conditions for women
- emigration

Essential Academic Vocabulary (Huntley, 2006, pages 120–121, 128–129)

List three ways that advanced level readers benefit from activities such as those you see above from *Essential Academic Vocabulary* in Example 4.

1. _____

2. _____

3. _____

Share your response with a colleague. What do you learn from your colleague's response?

_____

_____

_____

Compare your answers with ideas presented in the next three paragraphs.

_____

There are many ways that learners at the advanced level of proficiency benefit from vocabulary activities like those illustrated in Example 4. Let me share with you three direct benefits that I see. First, the readers encounter the vocabulary in a meaningful context. Having the context is always a useful way to learn new vocabulary.

A second benefit that I see from the way that Huntley treats the vocabulary is how she treats teaching the prefix *trans-*, providing eight words that use the prefix and looking at the meanings of the words.

A third benefit I see from Example 4 is how the parts of speech (nouns, verbs, adverbs, adjectives) are covered so that for a single word, other parts of speech are identified (i.e., as in exercise 6B in Example 4).

In *Focus on Vocabulary* (Example 5), Schmitt and Schmitt (2005) provide thematically organized units with four chapters per unit. Each chapter is divided into seven sections: getting started, target words, a reading, word meanings, word families, collocation exercises, and expansion activities.

Example 5

How Office Space Affects Behavior

GETTING STARTED

Discuss the following questions with your classmates.

▶ Where do you work best? Do you like to study in the privacy of your own room? Or are you happier in the library with a group of friends around you?

▶ What conditions are important for you to work well? What makes your study space comfortable?

▶ How important is it for you to interact with others to complete your assignments?

TARGET WORDS—Assessing Your Vocabulary Knowledge

Look at each of the target words in the box. Use the scale to give yourself a score for each word. After you finish the chapter, score yourself again to check your improvement.

1 I don't know this word.

2 I have seen this word before, but I am not sure of the meaning.

3 I understand the word when I see it or hear it in a sentence, but I don't know how to use it in my own speaking and writing.

4 I know this word and can use it in my own speaking and writing.

TARGET WORDS

_____administrative	_____considerable	_____exclusion	_____restrict
_____allocate	_____cycle	_____facilitate	_____seek
_____approach	_____debate	_____flexibility	_____status
_____assign	_____decade	_____maximum	_____trace
_____code	_____eliminate	_____percent	_____traditional
_____concentration	_____enhanced	_____phase	_____widespread

The following passage is adapted from an introductory textbook on management. This section focuses specifically on the relationship between work space and employee behavior. As you read, pay special attention to the target vocabulary words in **bold**.

Work Space Design

1 Businesses large and small now realize that physical work space influences employee behavior. As a result, businesses are redesigning their buildings and workplaces with the intent of reshaping employee attitudes and behavior. As firms redesign their offices, they focus on three main factors that have a strong impact on employee behavior: how much space employees have, how the space is arranged, and how much privacy employees have.

SIZE

2 In relation to work space, *size* is defined by the number of square feet per employee.

COLLOCATION

Each item below contains three sentences with the same collocation. Write a fourth sentence of your own using the same word partners.

1. **a.** Relief organizations aim to help people in developing countries **allocate** limited **resources** to long-term development projects like farming.
   b. The principal **allocated** equipment and **resources** equally between girls' and boys' sports teams.
   c. In the army, it is the job of the quartermaster to ensure that **resources** such as food and clothing are **allocated** efficiently.
   d. _____

2. **a.** The company's **practical approach** to employee training included offering workshops on new software applications.
   b. Workers must take a **practical approach** to balancing career and family life.
   c. Many hospital emergency rooms use a very **practical approach** called *triage* to ensure that the most seriously ill or injured patients are treated first.
   d. _____

3. **a.** Handling the airplane during the stormy weather required all of the pilot's **powers of concentration**.
   b. These works of philosophy ask too much of the students' **powers of concentration**.
   c. The speaker needed all of his **powers of concentration** to continue his talk after the demonstrators entered the auditorium.
   d. _____

4. **a.** An **ongoing debate** between environmentalists and traffic planners concerns whether more roads actually reduce traffic problems.
   b. Recent research into ape language has refuelled the **ongoing debate** about language being a uniquely human capability.
   c. The real reasons for global warming will continue to be the subject of **ongoing debate** by scientists for many years to come.
   d. _____

5. **a.** Digital technology has **greatly enhanced** the fields of photography, video, and broadcasting.
   b. Recipients of artificial hips normally find that their mobility is **greatly enhanced** after the operation.
   c. Lighter building materials have **greatly enhanced** the speed and capabilities of modern aircraft.
   d. _____

Focus on Vocabulary (Schmitt & Schmitt, 2005, pp. 70–71, 76–78)

Write three similarities and three differences you see between the exercises outlined in Example 5 from *Focus on Vocabulary* on pages 109–110 and the exercise in Example 4 from *Essential Academic Vocabulary* on pages 105–107. Which text do you think you would prefer for teaching advanced learners? Why?

Similarities

1. _____

2. _____

3. _____

Differences

1. _____

2. _____

3. _____

Reasons for preference

1. _____

2. _____

3. _____

Compare your similarities and differences with ideas presented below.

Three similarities that I see include (1) the vocabulary is placed in a meaningful context, (2) the authors provide opportunities to work with the vocabulary in skills other than reading, and (3) both books provide opportunities to practice using the vocabulary beyond the typical exercises.

Three differences that I noted between the two textbooks include (1) Schmitt and Schmitt provide the learner with an opportunity to self-assess their current knowledge of the target words, (2) Huntley provides work with the prefix, and (3) Schmitt and Schmitt teach the collocations of the target vocabulary.

Each of these books provides strong learning opportunities for learners at the advanced level of language proficiency to engage with academic vocabulary in meaningful ways.

3. Reading strategies and tasks

One very valuable reading strategy at the advanced level of reading is to use **graphic organizers**. A graphic organizer allows the reader to make a visual representation of the relationships among ideas in the text. Example 5 comes from *Quest 3, Reading and Writing*, 2nd ed. The reading from Unit

1 (Anthropology), Chapter 1 (Cultural Anthropology) is entitled "San Francisco Legislator Pushes *Feng Shui* Building Codes." The passage focuses on legislation introduced in the California legislature in 2004 to encourage building codes to include Chinese principles of *feng shui* to take advantage of the flow of energy.

The exercise illustrated in Example 6 focuses on using information from a specific paragraph in the reading to create a cause/effect graphic organizer.

Example 6

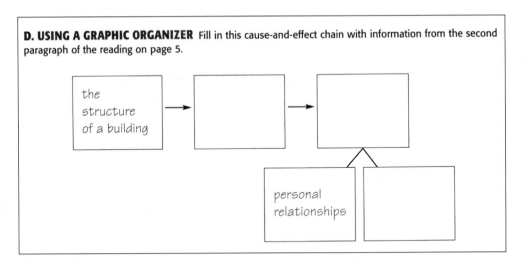

> ## Reading Strategy
>
> ### Using a Graphic Organizer to Show Cause and Effect
>
> When you put information into a **graphic organizer**, you can use the organizer to clearly **depict** (show) information. Graphic organizers help you see the relationships or connections among different ideas.
>
> When you organize information from readings in graphic organizers, you can then use them to review and study for exams. There are different types of graphic organizers, and you will work with many of them in this book.
>
> One type of graphic organizer depicts a **chain** of causes and effects. In other words, one situation (a cause) leads to another situation (the effect), which, **in turn**, becomes the cause of another effect. The graphic organizer on page 8 is a cause-and-effect chain.

D. USING A GRAPHIC ORGANIZER Fill in this cause-and-effect chain with information from the second paragraph of the reading on page 5.

the structure of a building → →

personal relationships

Quest 3, Reading and Writing, 2nd ed. (Hartmann and Blass, 2007, pages 7–8)

This exercise illustrates one way to help readers become more responsible for their reading and more conscious of the strategies that they use while engaged in reading. By creating a graphic organizer, readers can demonstrate that they see the relationships among the ideas presented in the text.

The second paragraph from the reading, "San Francisco Legislator Pushes *Feng Shui* Building Codes," is provided below. Read the paragraph and complete the graphic organizer below. Compare your graphic organizer with the one provided on page 128.

"Yee's office explains, 'The structure of a building can influence a person's mood, which can influence a person's behavior, which, in turn, can determine the person's personal and professional relationships. The aim of *feng shui* architecture is to study how the environment in which people live may affect their lives and influence their quality of life.'" (*Quest 3, Reading and Writing*, 2nd ed., Hartmann and Blass, 2005, page 5)

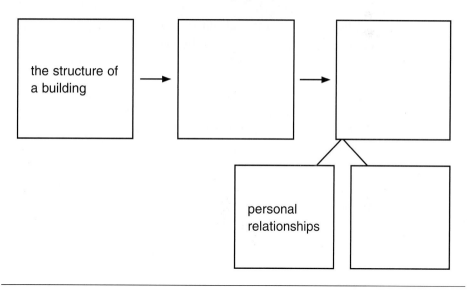

Also, by creating the graphic organizer, the reader is doing something with the information that was read. The graphic organizer is then a very good tool that the student can use to write or speak about the important relationships read from the text.

Create a reading lesson plan that incorporates the use of a cause/effect graphic organizer.

Share your lesson plan with a colleague.

4. Fluent reading tasks

Example 7 from *More Reading Power,* 2nd edition, provides excellent practice opportunities for readers to practice reading fluency. The authors suggest four steps for faster reading: (1) Check your reading habits. (2) Skip over unknown words. (3) Do reading sprints. (4) Practice reading faster by timing yourself. These suggestions, along with regular practice, can help readers with the goal of becoming more fluent readers.

This part of *More Reading Power* provides 30 passages, each approximately 500 words in length, for practice opportunities. Recall the definition of reading fluency used throughout this book: reading at an appropriate rate (200 wpm) with adequate comprehension (70 percent). In addition to checking reading rate, *More Reading Power* provides comprehension checks for each passage. Reading rate is recorded on a graph. Unfortunately, a comprehension graph is not provided.

Teachers can gather reading rates and comprehension scores from each student and calculate a class average. By sharing the class averages, progress can be measured as a group instead of as individuals.

Example 7

UNIT 1   Maria Montessori

Time yourself as you read the following passages. Read each passage and answer the questions on the following page. Do not look back at the passage as you answer the questions.

1. Childhood   Starting time _____

When Maria Montessori was born in Italy in 1870, her future seemed certain. Women did not have careers in those days, nor did they attend college. People generally believed that women were not very intelligent and not capable of complex thought, so Maria, it seemed, had little choice. Like her mother and most women of her day, she would become a mother and a housewife.

She did, in fact, become a mother, but otherwise, her life took a very different course. She became a doctor—the first woman doctor in Italy. With her brilliant medical studies and research, she proved that women could indeed think and work as well as men. Later, she became internationally famous as the inventor of the Montessori method of teaching. To this day, Montessori schools around the world f[...]

She was born in Chiaravalle, near Ancona, Italy[...] a government official in the state-run tobacco indu[...] liberation and unification of Italy. Well-educated hi[...] daughter. However, he was also conservative and di[...] Only later, when she became famous, did he chang[...]

Maria's mother never had any doubts about her[...] decisions and helped her through many difficult ti[...] but she wanted her daughter's life to be different. I[...] and the ideals necessary for success. She also taugh[...] Even as a small girl, Maria always had her share of [...] mother gave her a sense of responsibility toward ot[...] her later work as a doctor and as an educator.

The Montessori family moved several times wh[...] five, they went to live in Rome, and there she starte[...] student at that time, Maria did not seem very ambi[...] competitive behavior of some of her classmates. W[...] was for good behavior. In second grade, she won a[...] So far, her interests and achievements were the sam[...]

However, something in Maria's character stood [...] was often the leader in their games. Self-confident [...] that her life was somehow going to be different. At [...] dangerously ill, that belief in herself was already str[...] die because she had too much to do in life.

Finishing time[...]

Circle the best answer for each item. Do not look back at the passage.

1. This passage is about
   a. Maria Montessori's parents.
   b. girls in the nineteenth century.
   c. Maria Montessori's background and childhood.
   d. Maria Montessori's education.

2. We can infer from this passage that before Maria,
   a. many Italian women had studied medicine.
   b. Italian women didn't go to doctors.
   c. Italian women often became lawyers.
   d. no Italian women had ever studied medicine.

3. Maria Montessori
   a. was like most other women of her time.
   b. did not attend college.
   c. became a mother and a housewife.
   d. was not like most other women of her time.

4. Maria's father
   a. worked as a government official.
   b. ran a tobacco company.
   c. worked in a hospital.
   d. was an officer in the army.

5. The most important influence on Maria's development was probably her
   a. teacher.
   b. mother.
   c. father.
   d. illness.

6. Maria's mother believed in
   a. hard work and helping others.
   b. leaving the work for others.
   c. giving others hard work to do.
   d. helping her husband at work.

7. In primary school, Maria was
   a. a very brilliant student.
   b. a most unusual girl.
   c. not a very brilliant student.
   d. a terrible student.

8. As a child, Maria felt that
   a. her life was going to be short.
   b. she was going to be different from others.
   c. she was going to be just like others.
   d. her life was going to be very long.

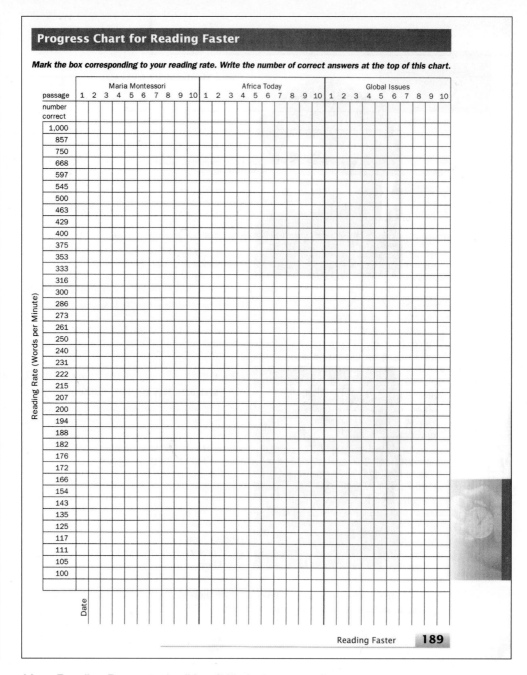

Progress Chart for Reading Faster

Mark the box corresponding to your reading rate. Write the number of correct answers at the top of this chart.

passage	Maria Montessori										Africa Today										Global Issues									
	1	2	3	4	5	6	7	8	9	10	1	2	3	4	5	6	7	8	9	10	1	2	3	4	5	6	7	8	9	10
number correct																														
1,000																														
857																														
750																														
668																														
597																														
545																														
500																														
463																														
429																														
400																														
375																														
353																														
333																														
316																														
300																														
286																														
273																														
261																														
250																														
240																														
231																														
222																														
215																														
207																														
200																														
194																														
188																														
182																														
176																														
172																														
166																														
154																														
143																														
135																														
125																														
117																														
111																														
105																														
100																														

Reading Rate (Words per Minute)

Date

Reading Faster **189**

More Reading Power, 2nd edition (Mikulecky and Jeffries, 2005, pp. 191, 192, 189)

Identify three ways in which *More Reading Power* provides practice in reading fluency.

1. _____

2. _____

3. _____

Do you have additional ideas of ways to help readers develop this important skill?

_____

_____

_____

_____

_____

Compare your ideas with those presented below.

_____

I have found that a book like *More Reading Power* is an excellent supplement for the reading classroom. Three ways that this textbook provides practice in reading fluency are (1) there are several passages at the same level of reading difficulty that can be used for fluency practice, (2) the passages are longer than the passages found in many reading textbooks so they provide opportunities for extensive reading, and (3) students have an opportunity to record their words-per-minute and track their progress.

The more opportunities we give learners, especially those at the advanced level, to practice reading fluency, the better readers they will become.

5. Reading inside and outside of the classroom

Providing meaningful reading opportunities both inside and outside of the classroom for advanced level readers is particularly important. Recall Figure 1–the learning/reading continuum (page 93). Readers at this level are very anxious to be able to move into interesting and motivating texts. They want to explore beyond the texts that are used for classroom instruction.

What meaningful connections do you think teachers can make between reading done inside class and reading done outside class? Do you think this is particularly important? Why or why not?

Share your answers with a classmate or colleague.

At this level, teachers are able to expose students to more content-area reading opportunities. The one thing that I have done to make this connection is to invite students to go to a university/college bookstore or a library and find an academic textbook in the field that they hope to study when they complete their English study. I ask them to read the introduction to the textbook and then come to class prepared to discuss the information. I group students by similar textbook topics if possible, and ask them to discuss what they learned from the introduction of the textbook.

What I have learned from doing this activity is that textbooks across academic content areas approach the introductions similarly. There is an introduction to how the textbook is organized. The authors provide valuable study tips. As we review the information together, I am able to point out to students that no matter what the textbook is, the organization and approach to the book will be similar across fields of study.

I then make sure, no matter what skill we are practicing in class—learning vocabulary from context, identifying main ideas, identifying rhetorical styles—that during the outside reading, the students are practicing these things. Students come to class with their textbooks ready to provide examples of how they have practiced outside of class the skills we are learning inside class.

This activity has been particularly motivating for my students. They see that there is a direct connection between what we do in class and what they do outside of class. This activity has helped students to pay close attention in class and to want to read outside of class.

Another important aspect of reading inside and outside of the classroom is the opportunity to engage meaningfully in reading for pleasure. No matter what the professional, vocational, or academic pursuits of our students, we can engage them in reading for fun. We can encourage students to read the newspaper, magazines, and books. We can have discussions in class about current events in the world and then read different perspectives on those events and compare and contrast the ideas of others.

A goal that every teacher of reading should set is to determine how to build a culture of reading by encouraging students to read both inside and outside of the classroom. By linking the two pedagogically, we will help students learn the value of reading in a wide variety of contexts.

6. Assessing advanced readers

Assessing readers at the advanced level of language proficiency is as important as assessing beginning and intermediate level learners. Learners at the advanced level are anxious to receive input from their teachers to know how they are doing. Regular in-class assessments are vital.

Recall that in this chapter, I have emphasized that learners are moving further to the right on the learning/reading continuum. (See Figure 1 page 93.) One trap that some teachers fall into is forgetting that learners at this level are still learning how to read. Teachers often assume that their students are only reading to learn. Unless we are teaching in a content-based instructional program, we do not want the focus of our assessments to cross the language learning/content learning boundary. Keep your assessments focused on learning the language and not learning the content.

We saw good examples of possible assessments in Examples 4 and 5 on pages 105 and 109 from Huntley (2006) and Schmitt and Schmitt (2005). There is a clear focus in each of these books on learning vocabulary and reading skills. There is a clear focus on integrating the learning from the reading with other language skills (listening, speaking, and writing). The focus is not on the content (economics, psychology, or political science) but on learning language.

There are many aspects of assessment that could be addressed at this level of proficiency. I want to focus our attention on assessment of vocabulary growth. I want to share information about two interesting websites that can be used for assessment of vocabulary as well as give an example of a vocabulary test.

Example 8

The Lexxica Word Engine (www.lexxica.com) is a particularly interesting website. First, the site is free to teachers and students. Second, there are four sections of the website that are valuable for students. (1) V-Check provides an accurate and reliable vocabulary test. The test is extremely simple. Readers are asked to answer *yes* or *no* to indicate they know the word. A score is then provided that gives the reader an approximation of vocabulary size. (2) The site provides V-Flash, which creates electronic flashcards that readers can use to practice vocabulary words. Vocabulary games are also featured on this part of the site. (3) V-Lexx provides graded stories and introduces a wide range of books and DVDs that learners can read and/or listen to. This section is particularly valuable since readers can target reading material that is within their vocabulary range. (4) V-Admin allows learners to organize V-Check scores and monitor progress.

My students at the advanced level found this website particularly inter-esting. First, they were all very anxious to learn the approximate size of their vocabulary. Second, the flashcards provided electronic opportunities to practice new vocabulary. They also found the graded reading texts helpful in targeting their level and providing meaningful reading practice.

Another valuable website for teachers is hosted on the University of Victoria's website (web.uvic.ca/~gluton/awl/). This site was developed with the sublists from the Academic Word List. I have assigned my advanced level class to work with a different AWL sublist each week. Students used this site as one of the practice activities prior to the weekly AWL test. The AWL sublist is subdivided further into six practice lists. Each of these six practice lists provides three practice exercises, which my students particularly like. I required that the student receive a score of 70 percent or higher on one exercise. If a score was below 70 percent, the students had to complete the next exercise. Students were motivated to study their own flashcards prior to engaging in the exercises on this list so that they would only have to complete one exercise.

The last example I would like to provide for assessing advanced level readers is an example of the weekly tests I gave on the AWL. Example 9 on pages 122–123 is a quiz I prepared for AWL sublist 10.

Action

Complete the vocabulary quiz in Example 8. As you are taking the quiz, make a list of the strategies that you are using as you answer each of the questions. Make a list of your reading strategies below.

1. _____

2. _____

3. _____

4. _____

Correct your responses with the answer key provided at the end of this chapter on page 128.

Example 9

Quiz – AWL 10

Fill in the gap

Each word is only used once. There are more words than there are possible sentences.

albeit	assemble	colleague	compile	depression
enormous	forthcoming	integrity	levies	likewise
odd	panel	persist	so-called	whereby

1. It is necessary for us to attend the lecture _____ difficult to be at class at 8:00 A.M.

2. Professor Shu has always maintained a high level of _____.

3. The government charged _____ against the illegal immigrants before deporting them.

4. _____ is a serious illness among many college-aged students.

5. The professor encouraged JZ to _____ in his study of academic vocabulary.

6. This is a very _____ request. Will you be able to meet me at the lecture hall at 5:30 tomorrow morning?

7. The Constitution of the United States guarantees that we have the right to _____ freely.

8. The professor asked that we _____ a list of all of the supplies we need to carry out the biology experiment.

9. Professor Hu is a _____ of Professor Lin.

10. Danilo wanted to get a degree in biology, so we agreed on a system _____ he could earn credit for taking the biology class at the ELC.

Sentences

Use each word in a **sentence**. The sentence must have at least five words and must be grammatically correct to get full points.

11. adjacent _____

12. assemble _____

13. collapse _____

14. compile _____

15. convince _____

16. encounter _____

17. levy _____

18. ongoing _____

19. persist _____

20. straightforward _____

Definition

Write the **definition** for the following words.

21. conceive _____

22. enormous _____

23. incline _____

24. integrity _____

25. invoke _____

26. panel _____

27. pose _____

28. reluctance _____

29. undergo _____

30. whereby _____

I designed this quiz in three parts. First, from a bank of words, readers are to complete a sentence with the correct word. Next, readers are to use each word in a sentence. Note that the sentence must have at least five words and must be grammatically correct to get full points. By encouraging length and grammatical accuracy, I was able to focus my students on more than just the isolated vocabulary word. Finally, students were to provide a definition for selected words from the AWL list.

This assessment looks very simple, but my students found it challenging. They were required to go beyond the simple vocabulary test of multiple choice or indicating if they knew the word or not. The test was productive. Giving the definitions and producing sentences of their own pushed the students to study the vocabulary more.

These three examples provide ways that teachers can incorporate vocabulary assessment meaningfully into classroom instruction to strengthen both teaching and learning.

Action

What other ways could you test the vocabulary skills of advanced level readers that you work with or might work with?

_____

_____

_____

_____

_____

Share your answers with a classmate or colleague.

_____

7. Conclusion

In this chapter, we have focused on six areas. First, we compared the CEF descriptors for beginning, intermediate, and advanced level readers. This description allowed us to see how readers at the advanced level differ from those at lower levels of language proficiency.

Second, we focused on syllabus design issues. Knowing whether the textbook or curricular goals drive the syllabus is important for teachers to know. Also, we reviewed the learning/reading continuum. Readers at this level of language proficiency are moving closer to the right end of the continuum: reading to learn. This section of the chapter also provided the opportunity to focus on the importance of integrating reading with other language skills.

Third, we identified five important principles that can guide our work with readers at the advanced level of language proficiency: (1) integrating reading with other language skills by placing reading at the core, (2) helping readers improve vocabulary skills through academic vocabulary instruction, (3) focusing on academic reading strategies to help advanced readers take responsibility for their own learning, (4) teaching advanced readers how reading on the computer is different from reading print material, and

(5) ensuring that readers at the advanced level of language proficiency are reading fluently.

Next, we examined examples from current textbooks of various tasks and activity types that illustrate the principles we have learned in this chapter: (1) integration of language skills, (2) vocabulary instruction, (3) academic reading strategies, (4) academic content, and (5) fluent reading.

Fifth, we noted that working with students with academic textbooks for reading outside the classroom can be connected to skills being taught inside the classroom.

Finally, we concluded the chapter with a discussion of assessing vocabulary skills for readers at this level.

This chapter provides valuable information on how to work with readers at the advanced level of proficiency. Following these ideas can lead to great success as we help readers make improvements in their reading skills.

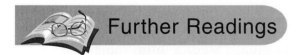 Further Readings

Field, M.L. 2006. Finding a Path to Fluent Academic and Workplace Reading. In E. Uso-Juan and A. Martinez-Flor (Eds.) *Current Trends in the Development and Teaching of the Four Language Skills* (pp. 329–354). New York, NY: Mouton de Gruyter.

Field discusses what makes a fluent reader and the barriers to fluent reading in an L2 setting, including issues of cultural identity in language use, vocabulary acquisition, and the need for level-appropriate materials to build confidence.

Rasinski, T., C. Blachowicz, & K. Lems (Eds.) 2006. *Fluency Instruction: Research-based best practices.* New York, NY: The Guilford Press.

This book considers the teaching of fluency in a variety of contexts, including literacy instruction, elementary classrooms, and teaching struggling readers.

Samuels, S.J. and A.E. Farstrup. 2006. (Eds.) *What Research Has to Say about Fluency Instruction.* Newark, DE: International Reading Association.

Samuels and Farstrup provide a history of developing research into fluency, as well as practical guides to measurement and assessment and to building fluency in the classroom. Special consideration is given to teaching students with dyslexia in an L2 context.

Taylor, A., J.R. Stevens, and J.W. Asher. 2006. The Effects of Explicit Reading Strategy Training on L2 Reading Comprehension: A meta-analysis. In J.M. Norris & L. Ortega (Eds.) *Synthesizing Research on Language Learning and Teaching* (pp. 213–244). Philadelphia, PA: John Benjamins Publishing Co.

This is a detailed examination of factors that can affect the teaching of cognitive and meta-cognitive teaching strategies. The authors show that students given explicit strategy instruction consistently outperform those who receive no such instruction.

Helpful Websites

Graphic.org (www.graphic.org/goindex.html)

Graphic.org provides a thematically organized directory of various types of graphic organizers.

The North Central Regional Educational Library (www.ncrel.org/ sdrs/areas/issues/students/learning/lr1grorg.htm)

The North Central Regional Educational Library also provides a directory of graphic organizers, and includes lesson plans with suggestions on how to use each type to strengthen learning.

Massey University School of Language Studies (http://language. massey.ac.nz/staff/awl/awlinfo.shtml)

The university gives information and background on Averil Coxhead's Academic Word List. A sublist of the most frequent headwords can be downloaded, and the complete AWL can be ordered electronically.

Vocabulary Exercises for the Academic Word List (web.uvic. ca/~gluton/awl)

Hosted by the University of Victoria, this page provides a bank of vocabulary activities based on the most frequently used word families in the AWL.

The Lexxica Word Engine (www.lexxica.com)

A free online site for vocabulary and reading practice, it is useful for both teachers and learners.

References

Anderson, N. J. 2003. Scrolling, Clicking, and Reading English: Online reading strategies in a second/foreign language. *The Reading Matrix, 3*(3).

Anderson, N. J. 2006. *ELT Advantage: Teaching ESL/EFL reading.* Boston: Thomson ELT. Available online at http://www.ed2go.com/eltadvantage

Bikowski, D. and G. Kessler. 2002. Making the Most of the Discussion Boards in the ESL classroom. *TESOL Journal, 11*(3), 27–29.

Coxhead, A. 2000. A New Academic Word List. *TESOL Quarterly, 34,* 213–238.

Council of Europe. 2001. *Common European Framework of Reference for Languages: Learning, Teaching, Assessment.* Cambridge, UK: Cambridge University Press.

Ediger, A.M. 2006. Developing strategic L2 readers… by reading for authentic purposes. In E. Uso-Juan, and A. Martinez-Flor (Eds.) *Current Trends in the Development And Teaching of the Four Language Skills (Studies on Language Acquisition)* (pp. 303–328). New York, NY: Mouton de Gruyter

Gunderson, L. 1991. *ESL Literacy Instruction: A guidebook to theory and practice.* Englewood Cliffs, NJ: Prentice-Hall, Inc.

Hazenberg, S.H. 1996. Defining a Minimal Receptive Second-language Vocabulary for Non-native University Students: An empirical investigation. *Applied Linguistics, 17*(145–163).

Huntley, H. 2006. *Essential Academic Vocabulary: Mastering the complete academic word list.* Boston, MA: Houghton Mifflin Company.

Ioannou-Georgiou, S. 2002. Constructing Meaning with Virtual Reality. *TESOL Journal, 11*(3), 21–26.

Kurniawan, S.H. and P. Zaphiris. 2001. *Reading Online or On Paper: Which is faster?* Paper presented at the 9th International Conference on Human Computer Interaction.

Murray, D.E. and D. McPherson. 2005. *Navigating to Read–Reading to Navigate.* Sydney, Australia: National Centre for English Language Teaching and Research, Macquarie University.

Samuels, S.J. 2006. Reading Fluency: Its past, present, and future. In T. Rasinski, C. Blachowicz, and K. Lems. (Ed.) *Fluency Instruction: Research-based best practices* (pp. 7–20). New York, NY: The Guilford Press.

Schmitt, D. and N. Schmitt. 2005. *Focus on Vocabulary: Mastering the academic word list.* White Plains, NY: Longman.

Sheorey, R. and K. Mokhtari. 2001. Differences in the metacognitive awareness of reading strategies among native and non-native readers. *System,* 29(4), 431–449.

Sutherland-Smith, W. 2002. Integrating Online Discussion in an Australian Intensive English Language Course. *TESOL Journal, 11*(3), 31–35.

Tindale, J. 2005. Reading Print and Electronic Texts. In *Navigating to Read– Reading to Navigate.* Sydney, Australia: National Centre for English Language Teaching and Research, Macquarie University.

Warschauer, M. 1997. Computer-mediated Collaborative Learning: Theory and practice. *Modern Language Journal, 81,* 470–481.

Warschauer, M. 1999. *Electronic Literacies: Language, culture, and power in online education.* Mahwah, N.J.: Lawrence Erlbaum Associates.

Warschauer, M. 2002. Networking into Academic Discourse. *Journal of English for Academic Purposes, 1,* 45–48.

West, **M.** 1953. *A General Service List of English Words.* Ann Arbor, MI: The
University of Michigan Press.

Answer Key for Action Box on page 112.

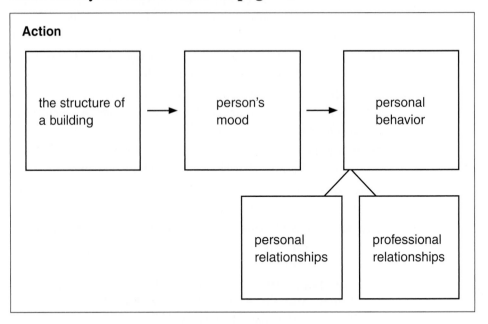

Answer Key Quiz – AWL 10 on page 122

Fill in the gap

Each word is only used once. There are more words than there are possible
sentences.

albeit	assemble	colleague	compile	depression
enormous	forthcoming	integrity	levies	likewise
odd	panel	persist	so-called	whereby

1. It is necessary for us to attend the lecture **albeit** difficult to be at class at
   8:00 A.M.
2. Professor Shu has always maintained a high level of **integrity**.
3. The government charged **levies** against the illegal immigrants before
   deporting them.
4. **Depression** is a serious illness among many college-aged students.
5. The professor encouraged JZ to **persist** in his study of academic
   vocabulary.
6. This is a very **odd** request. Will you be able to meet me at the lecture hall at
   5:30 tomorrow morning?
7. The Constitution of the United States guarantees that we have the right to
   assemble freely.

8. The professor asked that we **compile** a list of all of the supplies we need to carry out the biology experiment.
9. Professor Hu is a **colleague** of Professor Lin.
10. Danilo wanted to get a degree in biology, so we agreed on a system **whereby** he could earn credit for taking the biology class at the ELC.

Sentences

Use each word in a **sentence**. The sentence must have at least five words and must be grammatically correct to get full points. NOTE: Answers will vary from student to student.

11. adjacent	12. assemble	13. collapse	14. compile
15. convince	16. encounter	17. levy	18. ongoing
19. persist	20. straightforward		

Definition

Write the **definition** for the following words.

21. **conceive** – to form an idea or concept of something in your mind, to think up something that could be put into action
22. **enormous** – unusually large or great in size, amount, or degree
23. **incline** – to make somebody tend toward a particular belief or course of action
24. **integrity** – high moral principles or professional standards, the state of being complete or undivided
25. **invoke** – to call upon a greater power, to quote, rely on, to appeal for something
26. **panel** – a flat piece of wood, a display related to a computer screen, a group of people who publicly discuss a topic
27. **pose** – to adopt a physical posture for a photo, to pretend to be somebody or something else
28. **reluctance** – unwillingness or lack of enthusiasm, resistance
29. **undergo** – to experience or endure something or have something happen to you
30. **whereby** – by means of or through which

Chapter **Five**

Key issues in teaching reading

Goals

At the end of this chapter, you should be able to:

✔ **identify** five priorities for teachers of reading.

✔ **explain** the similarities and differences among key priorities recommended by four reading specialists.

✔ **explain** how you could implement the use of specific worksheets for explicitly teaching reading strategies.

✔ **explain** why bottom-up reading skills are so important to successful reading.

✔ **identify** how to explicitly teach reading fluency.

✔ **identify** how to use extensive reading effectively.

✔ **create** your own personal professional development plan to continue making improvements in your teaching of reading.

1. Introduction

The primary goal of this chapter is to assist you in becoming aware of key issues that are important for teachers of reading. To do this, we first examine lists of priorities for teachers of reading identified by four reading specialists and a group of EFL teachers from India. We then focus on five key issues that reading teachers should be very familiar with in order to be more effective in the classroom. The five areas of focus include: (1) the role of reading strategies, (2) the importance of bottom-up reading skills, (3) the need for both silent and oral reading fluency, (4) the need for more extensive reading, and (5) the need for professional development for teachers of reading.

2. Top-five lists of priorities for teachers of reading

It is impossible in a single book to address in adequate depth all of the things that second language teachers of reading should be aware of to be successful in the classroom. There are so many reference books and articles published annually that it is difficult to keep up with everything that is happening. However, we can learn from teachers and researchers who have been thinking about and addressing issues related to second language reading. This can assist us in our own development as teachers of reading.

Action

What do you believe are the top five priorities for you as a teacher of reading? List your priorities below.

1. _____

2. _____

3. _____

4. _____

5. _____

We will return to your list later in the chapter.

I invited four colleagues who have specialized in teaching and researching second language reading to each provide a list of the top five priorities they believe are important for second language teachers of reading to be aware of. We will now see what Julian Bamford, Lynn Erler, Bill Grabe, and Fredricka Stoller have each identified as five priorities for second language teachers of reading.

Julian Bamford's list

Julian Bamford teaches at Bunkyo University, Chigasaki, Japan. He is co-author of *Extensive Reading in the Second Language Classroom* (Cambridge University Press) and co-editor of *Extensive Reading Activities for Teaching Language* (also CUP).

1. The overriding priority for L2 (second language) reading teachers is seeing to it that the learners want to read in the L2. Reading is a skill that improves through practice. If learners don't want to read, they probably won't get the practice they need to become fluent, confident readers.

My other priorities are in service of the first. If we ask, "Why do learners *not* want to read?" the most common answer is, "It's too difficult." This produces priorities 2 and 3:

2. Learners need plenty of reading material that is very easy–either found material, or material written or edited for L2 learners at a particular proficiency level.

3. The reading material should be highly compelling–that is, relevant, interesting, and/or enjoyable to the learners.

And to attack the all-important difficulty problem from the other direction:

4. Students of reading should be learning the L2 so that more reading material becomes readable. Their particular need is a system for relentlessly building their vocabulary.

Learners also answer that they don't want to read because . . . they just don't feel like it. This leads to the final priority:

5. The learners and teacher should create a community of readers. Reading is usually a solitary activity, but a reader can benefit in all sorts of ways by sharing it with others. When others enjoy reading, they are role models for a learner to aspire to. Learners can share reactions, and recommend good reading material to each other.

The synergy of a shared endeavor greatly increases the chances that learners want to read. And so the reading teacher avoids the soul-destroying task of–in David Eskey's memorable metaphor–trying to teach swimming strokes to people who hate the water.

Lynn Erler's list

Dr. Lynn Erler works in reading research at Oxford University Department of Education in Oxford, England. Her interests are particularly in young adolescents' cognitive experiences of reading in a foreign language.

1. Tasks. The reading tasks we engage learners in should be varied, and teachers should understand both the purpose and the implications of the task in terms of required engagement by the reader with the text in order to do the task. What part(s) of the text need to be understood in order to achieve the task; what written language can be ignored when doing the task and is that really helpful for the learner? Is that what the teacher has in mind as the reading experience for the learner?

2. Interest and motivation. The reason(s) for reading as viewed by the teacher and also by the student; this should extend far beyond the task and should include the learner's personal interests and the teacher's solid understanding of what would or could motivate the reader to engage in all the language and meaning of a particular text.

3. L1 (first language). Teachers need to be aware of the role of the learners' L1 during L2 reading. This includes level of L1 literacy and aspects of L1 which cause interference. These could range from decoding problems to cultural misapprehensions about the schema of the text. Teachers should also be aware of which aspects of L1 knowledge and L1 literacy actually support the reader's understanding of the text, including translating from L2 to L1 either mentally or on paper. Teachers should give thought to how they can work with the reader to accommodate the L1 profitably, according to the individual reader's needs.

4. Level of L2. This is an obvious area for consideration: text level should not be too low, but some low-level, easier texts might be "refreshing" sometimes. The level should not be too high but there should be opportunities for learners to stretch themselves if they wish. This variety of opportunities has resource implications, i.e., have plenty on hand to read.

5. Strategies. Teachers need to know the strategies, including the various forms of avoidance and wild guessing, that students use with a text, and then decide on whether training of effective strategies is needed. If so, carrying out that training is recommended. Metacognitive strategies, particularly those of evaluating strategy employment and strategy effectiveness by the learner, must be part of the strategies program.

Bill Grabe's list

Bill Grabe is professor of English in the English department at Northern Arizona University in Flagstaff, Arizona, USA. He has served as the president of the American Association of Applied Linguistics. He is best known for his research on second language reading research and teaching.

1. Vocabulary. Knowing appropriate vocabulary in English is essential to good reading. Our knowledge and understanding of the role of vocabulary has increased significantly during the past 10 years. Explicit teaching of vocabulary and vocabulary learning strategies is an important role for teachers in the classroom.

2. Fluency, both sight word recognition speed and text reading fluency. Readers need to be reading at least 200 words per minute with 70 percent comprehension. A reading rate and comprehension level below this suggests that the reader is not a fluent reader. Regular, consistent instruction in the classroom is essential for learners to become fluent readers.

3. Discourse structure awareness. As learners become more fluent readers, an increased knowledge of the discourse structures in English becomes important. Awareness of the discourse structures in English helps readers read more fluently as well.

4. Strategic responses to difficult texts. Knowledge of appropriate reading strategies is vital for effective reading instruction. Readers need explicit instruction in reading strategies in order to become more aware of the options available to them when they encounter difficult texts.

5. Reading a lot. In order to become a better reader, learners must read a lot. Through reading a lot learners find vocabulary, the discourse structures, and the strategies they have been learning in shorter passages. Readers can also practice reading fluently. This final top-five suggestion provides the perfect opportunity to pull together the other four in a natural reading environment.

Fredricka Stoller's list

Fredricka L. Stoller is professor of English at Northern Arizona University in Flagstaff, Arizona, USA, where she teaches in the MA TESL and PhD in Applied Linguistics programs.

1. The best way to help students learn to read and improve their reading skills is through reading itself.

There is no substitute for the actual act of reading. Too often, so-called reading classes focus more attention on completing comprehension questions, discussing and writing about readings, and reviewing vocabulary. If reading improvement is a primary instructional objective, students should be engaged in as much reading as possible, in class and out of class.

2. Giving students choices in what they read can empower students and lead to more student engagement in reading.

Too often, teachers assign readings without giving students any choices whatsoever. Even though most of us teach in settings with mandated objectives and textbooks, it behooves us to reexamine our reading curricula to find opportunities for supplementary readings. The ideal is to give students some choices in the readings that they do. When given choices, students are likely to take the task more seriously and enjoy being a reader. After such reading assignments, student pairs and groups can be defined by true information gaps. Student readers are instantly "experts" and have something real to share with their classmates.

3. One of the best ways to inspire students to read and to grasp the excitement that is often associated with reading is for teachers to lead by example.

Many of our students come from environments void of reading materials and readers. Teachers should talk with their students about what they are reading and what they've learned from their reading. During sustained silent reading periods, teachers too should engage in reading, rather than taking that time to grade papers or plan future lessons.

4. One of the best ways to promote reading fluency and meaningful reading is through rereading.

Teachers often believe that the more reading passages they bring into class, the more effective their instruction is. In fact, it might be better to bring in fewer passages and exploit those that are assigned by asking students to reread them for different purposes (e.g., to identify the main idea, to find details, to determine the author's stance, to compare with another text). Each time through the passage, the student readers become more comfortable with the text, thereby building their confidence and self-esteem as readers.

5. Students most often rise or fall to the level of expectation of their teachers. Thus, teachers should set high expectations for all learners and assist them in achieving those expectations.

One way to help students become better, more confident readers, thereby meeting our expectations, is to help them develop into more strategic readers. Instead of simply asking students to practice different strategies in relative isolation, we teachers should engage students in discussions of why we are reading, what strategies we might use to meet our objectives, and when and how we might use those strategies. Conversing about strategies—to answer *which, when, why,* and *how* questions—followed up by meaningful practice, is likely to give students the tools needed to meet our high expectations and become more skilled and confident readers.

List of priorities from EFL teachers in India

While working on this chapter, I was working with a group of English teachers in India with a focus on teaching reading. I asked them the same question that I asked the ESL/EFL specialists. In India, I gathered input from 36 teachers. These teachers taught a wide range of English language learners. Some taught primary school learners, others taught secondary school learners, and some taught adult learners. But you will note that their priorities apply to learners at any age level and to any level of language proficiency. I received over 100 suggestions of priorities that this group of teachers thought were important for teachers to be aware of while teaching reading. I consolidated the list and provide for you here the top-five responses given by this group of teachers.

1. **Reading purpose.** Why are the students reading the text? What is it that the teacher hopes the students will learn from the text? The teacher must know before asking students to read what the purpose of the text is. Knowing the reading purpose will improve the use of class time.

2. **Comprehension.** It is important to remember that the overall goal of reading is comprehension. Students must be taught how to understand different parts of a text and what to do when they do not understand.

3. **Vocabulary knowledge.** Students should not get bogged down with difficult words. Help students know how to either skip unknown words or to use the context to guess the meaning.

4. **Repeated reading.** With each reading of a text, students will learn more and make improvements. Use each text for more than one reading.

5. **Pronunciation and oral reading fluency.** Students should be instructed on how to read aloud in a strong voice with good pronunciation and fluency. Strong oral reading is characteristic of a good reader.

Action

What similarities and differences do the five lists have? Make a list below of the similarities and differences.

Similarities

_____

_____

_____

_____

_____

Differences

_____

_____

_____

_____

Compare your list with a classmate's or colleague's. Then compare your lists with the information presented below.

From this list of 25 priorities, there is overlap in eight of the ideas: (1) reading a lot of material, (2) the role of vocabulary, (3) the role of strategies, (4) the need to reread texts, (5) reading fluency, (6) motivation, (7) interest, and (8) level of difficulty of the material. These are each ideas that can serve a teacher well in preparing to be a better teacher of reading.

Ten ideas from these five lists are not shared. (1) teacher example, (2) setting high expectations, (3) providing choice in the selection of reading materials, (4) creating a community of readers, (5) the role of the L1, (6) reading tasks, (7) discourse structure awareness, (8) reading purpose, (9) the role of comprehension, and (10) pronunciation and oral fluency.

Action

Return to the list of priorities that you made on page 131. How similar and different is the list of your priorities with those we have discussed above? What changes would you make in your list now that you have seen the lists of others? Make note of those changes below.

1. _____

2. _____

3. _____

4. _____

5. _____

We will return to this revised list later in the chapter.

As a profession, can teachers or a professional association reduce all of our knowledge of the teaching of reading down to just five priorities? I don't think so. Also, as we work with students from different language backgrounds (i.e., in an ESL setting), or students of different ages or proficiency levels, can we reduce the required knowledge down to just five priorities? I don't think so. Should teachers identify their own list of five priorities that should guide them in their teaching of reading? Absolutely! Will that list of priorities stay the same over the career of a teacher? No! The list will evolve and change as we evolve and change as teachers.

I believe that the important thing is that as teachers of reading, we have thought through what issues should be priorities for us as individual teachers and that we are working on improving our teaching. We will address more specific ways that this can be done in the final section of this chapter.

In this first part of the chapter, we have reviewed a variety of priorities that teachers should be aware of as they engage in the teaching of reading. In the following five sections, I share with you my top five priorities that I believe every second language teacher should know about L2 reading. Is my list better than your list or the lists provided above? Certainly not. These are priorities that I believe in and share with teachers on things that can be done to improve reading instruction. My list includes:

1. the role of reading strategies
2. the importance of bottom-up reading skills
3. the need for both silent and oral reading fluency
4. the need for more extensive reading
5. the need for professional development for teachers of reading

3.   The role of reading strategies

In Chapters 2, 3, and 4 we identified strategies that learners at the beginning, intermediate, and advanced levels of language proficiency should be aware of. For example in Chapter 4 (p. 98), I provided a list from Gunderson (1991) of 34 content reading strategies that are valuable to explicitly teach to advanced level readers. Perhaps the most important message I want to convey in this chapter is that explicit strategy instruction does not just happen by itself. Teachers must be prepared with a plan for how they are going to explicitly teach reading strategies to the students they work with. Recall that in Section 2, Erler, Grabe, and Stoller all listed reading strategies and strategic reading among their priorities for reading teachers.

If our goal is to develop readers who are aware of their strategies and readers who are doing everything they can to take control of their own learning, we must have teachers who are guiding them in the initial stages of that awareness. Awareness of reading strategies is part of the group of **metacognitive strategies**.

Reading purpose is central to the selection and use of strategies. One of the first things that teachers can do to help learners be more strategic readers is to verify that they understand their purpose for reading. Identifying a reading purpose prior to actually reading is central to reading success. For example, when reading a newspaper, a reader may have the purpose of reading to find out the details of a current event. When reading a textbook, a reader may have the purpose of learning how to conduct an experiment. When reading a novel, a reader may have the purpose of simply enjoying the story. Whatever the purpose, it is important to know why you are reading.

Reading strategy instruction should always be integrated into the overall instruction. We cannot hope that readers will improve in their use of strategies if the strategies are simply addressed sporadically. Many reading textbooks, especially in EFL contexts, will not specifically address reading strategies.

Teachers can effectively integrate explicit strategy instruction into the reading materials that are currently used in the classroom. We saw examples of effective integration of strategy instruction in Chapter 2 (pages 40–42) with examples from *ReadSmart 1* (Pavlik, 2004), *ACTIVE Skills for Reading,* Book 1 (Anderson, 2007), and *Read and Reflect 1* (Adelson-Goldstein with Howard, 2004). Other examples are in Chapters 3 and 4 on pages 75, 105, and 112.

In each of these cases, the lessons have an explicit focus on the development of reading strategies.

Modeling by the teacher is essential to teaching reading strategies. As teachers model how to use the strategies effectively, readers will see how they can follow the teacher's example to get the greatest benefit out of the strategy. When I introduce a new strategy to students, I want them to watch me using the strategy. I also want the students to see which other strategies I combine with the specific strategy I am modeling.

For example, when I teach the strategy of predicting, I will read a text to the students and then pause and tell the students what I predict will happen in the reading or what I predict a certain outcome will be. I model other strategies like how the context helps me make the prediction. I also model confirming or rejecting the predictions I have made. In this way, the students see the strategies being used in my actual reading.

Metacognitive awareness is central to effective strategy instruction. Before they begin to read, learners should plan how to successfully accomplish their reading goal. Activation of prior knowledge is one way to plan. Readers can ask themselves what they know about what they are about to read. They can ask what they hope to learn. They can preview the text and read bold or italicized words or phrases and read any headings. If students are reading a novel, they should read the information on the back cover of the book and read information about the author.

Selecting which strategies to use for a particular reading task is another part of metacognitive awareness. Learners need opportunities to learn about the variety of reading strategies that are available for them to use. Good readers use a wide variety of strategies. Poor readers use a limited number of strategies. Our role as teachers is to help readers select, develop, and use strategies for becoming better readers. On page 98, a list of appropriate strategies was provided. Review that list for ideas of strategies to teach.

Once they begin a reading task, learners should monitor their own strategy use. Readers need to be taught to ask themselves whether the strategies they are using are effective for them. Not all strategies will work equally well for all learners. Monitoring strategy use provides the opportunity for readers to practice a variety of strategies and learn which are the best fit for their own learning style.

It is clear from all the literature on reading strategies that strategies are not used in isolation. Strategy clusters are used. For example, if readers make a prediction about what they anticipate will come in a text, a combination strategy will be to confirm or reject the prediction. Teachers can help readers see the clusters of strategies that will work for accomplishing their reading purpose.

After a reading task is completed, the use of metacognitive strategies continues. Learners need to be taught how to evaluate the effectiveness of the strategies they are using. After having opportunities to practice and certainly while engaged in a reading task, evaluation of strategy use is an important part of effective learning.

Managing My Own Learning (MMOL)

Kenton Harsch and Leslie Riley have developed a series of six worksheets that teachers can use to help learners monitor their own language learning experience. These forms are free and available to any interested language teacher. Go to http://www2.hawaii.edu/~kenton/srl/ to download the worksheets. (They are also included in Appendix 3 on pages 165–174.) Although not specifically developed for teaching and learning reading strategies, the worksheets can fit perfectly into a reading classroom. They make it particularly easy for a teacher to integrate explicit strategy instruction into their teaching.

Worksheet A, Introduction and Discussion (pages 165–167), provides a structured way for teachers to introduce learners to strategies. This introductory process allows learners to share with others what their beliefs are about language learning. The value of Worksheet A is that learners are able to identify what they expect a teacher to do and what they expect to do themselves. Strategy use cannot be dictated by teachers but must be developed and monitored by readers themselves. For this reason, it is very important to clarify from the beginning the expectations of both the teachers and the learners. You will notice that on many of the worksheets, students are asked to identify and think about the strategy clusters they are using instead of single strategies. This idea is introduced on Worksheet A.

Worksheet B (page 168) is the readers' personal strategy repertoire. This form allows readers to keep a list of the strategies they are naturally using or practicing. I ask students to use this worksheet as a daily record of the strategies we talk about in class as well as the strategies that they are using outside of class. This is a valuable worksheet for helping readers become more aware of the full range of strategies that they could use.

Worksheet C (page 169) provides readers the opportunity to reflect on the learning challenges that they have faced during the past week and describe what strategies they implemented to solve the learning problem. This worksheet is valuable for readers who are learning to monitor their strategy use.

Worksheet D (pages 170–171) is a synthesis of input from several Worksheet Cs, allowing readers to see what patterns are emerging in their individual strategy use. What I find particularly valuable about Worksheet D is that it helps readers to become researchers using their individual strategies as the data for responding to these questions.

Worksheet E (page 172) provides learners the opportunity to interview a classmate using their previous worksheet to answer the questions. By interviewing a classmate, learners have the opportunity to learn what other students do to solve language learning difficulties. Since no two readers are likely to solve the same problem in the same way, this is a valuable activity to help individuals see that there is more than one way to use strategies. I encourage readers to focus on the strategy clusters that they are using as they encounter reading challenges.

Worksheet F (page 173) is an optional activity that further encourages students to share the variety of strategies that they are using. Worksheet F guides learners through the process of preparing an oral presentation. The oral presentation provides a good opportunity to integrate speaking into the reading class. Students tell their classmates what works for them and what they are doing to become a better learner and reader.

Finally, Worksheet G (page 174) is another optional activity. This worksheet guides learners through the process of writing a newsletter to share with others about what individual students in a class are doing to be successful readers and take responsibility for their own learning. The newsletter is an authentic writing task in which current students write to other students or to future students about being good readers.

I have used these worksheets in my classes and have found that they make it very easy to introduce, model, monitor, and track explicit strategy instruction. Students look forward to opportunities to share with others and, perhaps equally as important, to learn from their classmates in this structured yet informal way.

Action

Review Worksheets A-G from Harsch and Riley (pages 165–174). List ways that you believe you could implement the use of these forms in your own teaching.

1. _____

2. _____

3. _____

4. _____

5. _____

Share your answers with a classmate or colleague.

I administer Worksheet A as a way to introduce the concept of language learning strategies and to encourage students to take charge of their own learning. I have the students complete the worksheet at the beginning of a course. I have also administered it at the end of a course to allow students to see how their answers have changed over time.

Worksheet B is one that I have students bring to class every day. As students share strategies they are using inside and outside of the class, I have them write the strategies on Worksheet B. I regularly have students use Worksheet B as part of a homework assignment, where I ask them to monitor their strategy use while reading and record what strategies they use.

I have students complete Worksheet C once a week. This worksheet encourages the students to think about the learning challenges they face and what they need to do in order to solve the problems. This worksheet allows me as the teacher to provide feedback and input–if specifically requested with a checkmark by the student on the worksheet–about their learning challenges. Worksheets D and E provide an opportunity for students to consolidate and synthesize information they have recorded on Worksheets B and C over a period of time. I have found these forms work well midway through a course and at the end of a course. The information students write here is one more source of input on how well they are taking responsibility for their learning. When students interview a classmate using Worksheet E they get input from others on what strategies others find helpful. A reader-to-reader conversation can often be more helpful than more input from me as a teacher.

Worksheets F and G are an excellent way to bring closure to the entire process. These worksheets allow learners to give oral presentations and create a newsletter that can be useful for other students. This also provides a meaningful way for students to write about the learning process and strategy use for an authentic audience (other students).

All six of the worksheets can be a structured, useful way to approach the teaching of strategies and to help learners understand the importance of taking responsibility for their own learning.

4. The importance of bottom-up reading skills

Recall the discussion from Chapter 1 on **bottom-up**, **top-down**, and **interactive models** of reading (pages 5–8). Bottom-up models of reading focus on the smallest units of meaning and build to larger units. Sounds build to letters, which build to words, phrases, sentences, and paragraphs. Also, recall that we emphasized in the earlier discussion that our instructional objective is to achieve a balanced approach to teaching reading, which would reflect an interactive model of reading instruction where both bottom-up and top-down skills are taught. I have found that in most reading textbooks and classrooms, the small units that comprised the bottom-up approach often get overlooked during reading instruction.

Birch (2007) provides a current perspective on the importance of bottom-up skills necessary for successful reading. She emphasizes that **phonological strategies, orthographic strategies, lexical strategies,** and **syntactic strategies** are all important for successful reading.

Given this information, teachers, curriculum developers, and program administrators must ask themselves what specific steps are taken to ensure that readers have a solid foundation of bottom-up reading skills. There are four primary reasons that bottom-up reading skills are so important to successful reading: (1) phonological strategies allow the reader to pronounce the word correctly, (2) orthographic strategies help readers decode new words they encounter, (3) lexical strategies allow readers to gain access to vocabulary that they have learned and connect the meanings of the word with the pronunciation of the word, and finally, (4) syntactic strategies allow the reader to connect the individual words into the appropriate order consistent with the rules of the language they are reading.

Each of these concepts is central to successful bottom-up reading skills. As mentioned earlier, these concepts are often overlooked in reading programs. The bottom-up skills for successful reading are natural ways that we can use reading as the core skill and link to other important language skills. Recall the discussion from Chapter 4 on how reading can be at the core of instruction (pages 95–96). We can easily link reading to speaking (phonological strategies), writing (orthographic strategies), and grammar (syntactic strategies).

Action

What are some specific ways you could better integrate bottom-up skills into reading instruction to strengthen the skills of ESL/EFL readers?

1. _____

2. _____

3. _____

4. _____

5. _____

Share your ideas with a classmate or colleague.

5. The need for both silent and oral reading fluency

Reading fluency has increased in importance in recent years, primarily because of two major reports that emphasized fluency: the National Reading Panel's report (Panel, 2000) and *Preventing Reading Difficulties in Young Children* (Snow, Burns, and Griffin, 1998). Each of these reports received wide distribution and each emphasized the essential role that reading fluency plays in successful reading. Hudson, Lane, and Pullen (2005) state that "reading fluency is one of the defining characteristics of good readers, and a lack of fluency is a common characteristic of poor readers" (p. 702).

In addressing reading fluency, two issues arise: first, fluency during silent reading and second, fluency during oral reading. Reading silently is the primary way that people engage in the act of reading. Far more people engage in silent reading than in oral reading. "Reading out loud with fluency (i.e., with purpose, speed, intonation, and comprehension) is of secondary importance for most students and their teachers. Automaticity should be the goal for reading instruction, and not oral fluency" (Birch, 2007). Individual teachers and reading programs need to consider specific goals for silent reading fluency. Teachers should determine exactly what they are going to do to help readers become more fluent, silent readers.

Action

What are some specific things that you could do in a reading classroom to practice silent reading fluency?

1. _____

2. _____

3. _____

4. _____

5. _____

Compare your list above with the information presented below.

One of the greatest challenges that teachers face is knowing exactly what pedagogical activities they can include in the classroom to help students increase their silent reading fluency. I encourage teachers to use five fluency activities regularly in the classroom: shadow reading, rate buildup reading, repeated reading, class-paced reading, and self-paced reading.

Shadow reading

First, I use the audio CD that accompanies the reading text that I use in class or if an audio CD is not available, I read the passage aloud. I have learners listen to the reading passage. I do not have them look at the printed text. They are asked to just listen. Following the listening passage, we discuss what we heard.

Next, after a brief discussion, I ask the readers to open their books and follow along silently as they listen to the recording again on the CD. For most of the learners in my class, their eyes are moving faster while following the text and listening to the recording than they would be if they were reading silently by themselves. This is a good practice opportunity. Students begin to realize that the rate of speech in listening is faster than they are accustomed to reading.

Finally, I have the learners read aloud quietly with the CD. Keeping up is often a challenge as learners are not accustomed to reading that fast orally. We may repeat this phase of shadow reading more than once during the lesson. Students enjoy the challenge of trying to keep up with the CD.

Following the shadow reading activity, readers will answer the reading comprehension questions that accompany the passage. By doing this, readers understand that they are responsible for comprehension as well as reading rate.

Rate buildup reading

Students are given 60 seconds to read as much material as they can. They then begin reading again from the beginning of the text and are again given 60 seconds. They are to read more material during the second 60-second period than in the first. The drill is repeated a third and a fourth time. The purpose of this activity is to reread "old" material quickly, gliding into the new. As the eyes move quickly over the "old" material, the students actually learn how to get their eyes moving at a faster reading rate. The exercise involves more than simply moving the eyes quickly—the material should be processed and comprehended. As students participate in this rate building activity, they learn to increase reading rate.

Repeated Reading

Repeated reading was first developed by Samuels (1979), and he continues to help teachers understand the importance of this classroom reading activity (Samuels, 2006).

In this technique, students read a short passage over and over again until they achieve criterion levels of reading rate and comprehension. For example, they may try to read a short 100-word paragraph four times in two minutes. The criterion levels may vary from class to class, but reasonable goals to work towards are criterion levels of 200 words per minute at 70 percent comprehension.

Class-paced reading

This activity requires a discussion regarding a class goal for minimal reading rate. Once that goal is established, the average number of words per page of the material being read is calculated. It is then determined how much material needs to be read in one minute in order to meet the class goal. For example, if the class goal is to read 250 wpm (words-per-minute) and the material being read has an average of 125 words per page, the class would be expected to read one page every 30 seconds. As each 30-second time period elapses, the teacher indicates to the class to move to the next page. Students are encouraged to keep up with the established class goal. Of course, those who read faster than 250 wpm are not expected to slow down their reading rate. As long as they are ahead of the designated page they continue reading.

Self-paced reading

The procedures for this activity are very similar to the class-paced reading activity outlined above. During this reading-rate activity, the students determine their own goal for reading rate. They then determine how much material needs to be read in a 60-second period to meet their objective rate. For example, suppose a student's reading rate objective is 180 words-per-minute and that the material being read has an average number of 10 words per line. The student would need to read 18 lines of text in one minute to meet the goal. The activity proceeds nicely by having each student mark off several chunks of lines and silently read for a period of five to seven minutes with the instructor calling out minute times. Students can then determine if they are keeping up with their individual reading rate goal.

These rate-building activities seek to get the readers to a level of automatic processing of the text. That is, reading and processing the text without anxiety about the meanings of individual words.

How is reading silently similar to and different from reading orally?

1. _____

2. _____

3. _____

4. _____

5. _____

Compare your list with the information presented below.

Fluent oral reading

In many parts of the world, the primary focus in reading instruction is oral reading. Oral reading is a social custom that began before books were easily available. One member of a family would read to the rest of the family, usually in the evening around the fire. The reader was expected to read with expression, inflection, and emotion. Good articulation was important. Reading orally continues to be important to many teachers and English language programs around the world. I suggest that in order to be a strong, fluent, oral reader, one must first be a strong, fluent *silent* reader.

There are six reasons why oral and silent reading are different in purpose and effect. First, the pedagogical goals for having students read aloud are different from the goals of reading silently. Second, when reading orally, more cognitive capacity is required and thus makes a focus on comprehension more challenging. Next, oral reading rate is dependent upon the speed at which one can talk. Silent reading can happen at much faster rates. Fourth, oral reading should be preceded by a stronger focus on bottom-up reading skills. Fifth, a fluent silent reader is a stronger oral reader. Sixth, there is also the issue of anxiety. Anxiety can increase with the feeling that the reader has to perform in front of one's peers and teacher.

Reason #1: Pedagogical goal

What is the reason that teachers ask students to read orally? The primary answer I get to this question when I ask teachers is that they want to ensure that students can pronounce words correctly, read in appropriate phrases, and read with proper intonation. I suggest that this is not a reading issue but rather an issue of improving speaking skills.

Recall the discussion from Chapter 4 on placing reading at the core of instruction and then building other skills (pages 95–96). It is very appropriate to build readers' speaking skills through reading. This is the perfect opportunity to teach students how to be strong readers and then teach them how to read orally what they can already read silently. Teaching correct pronunciation, phrasing, and intonation is a very appropriate speaking skill to build from reading.

Perhaps teachers should identify other tasks that they can engage in to check the pronunciation skills of learners instead of asking them to read. My greatest fear is that by asking students to engage in oral reading, we discourage students from developing their skills instead of encouraging and motivating them to become better readers.

If you are part of a program that encourages oral reading, verify the rationale for using oral reading. If the rationale is not directly related to helping learners become strong, more independent readers, consider other activities to engage learners in to test what you are seeking to test.

Reflection

Think about times you have had to read aloud. What has been difficult about that task? What has been rewarding?

Share your answers with a classmate or colleague.

Reason #2: Cognitive capacity and reading

When we engage in any thinking activity, we have a limited amount of capacity available to us. Readers who are still learning how to be good readers (orally or silently) are often distracted from the primary task of reading: achieving comprehension. The distractions can come from teachers who ask the students to do too many things at the same time.

How many of us have been asked to read aloud in our second language and then immediately asked to explain the meaning of what we have read or to explain why it is significant? I have found myself in this setting multiple times. The challenge is that when we are asked to read aloud, our cognitive capacity shifts from comprehension of what we are reading to making sure that we are reading aloud correctly. I find myself worrying that I am not reading loud enough for others to hear, that I am not reading the words correctly, and hoping that I don't come to a word that is difficult to pronounce. My cognitive capacity is used to focus on the oral aspects of reading and not on the comprehension of what I am reading.

If a reader is a strong, silent reader, then many of the cognitive factors that we have identified above are reduced. Strong, silent readers have more confidence and thus are not as worried about voice control and pronunciation when they read aloud.

If our goal is to produce strong, independent readers, let's ensure that we are structuring the reading tasks so that the learners' cognitive capacity can be dedicated to our primary focus: reading comprehension.

Reason #3: Oral and silent reading rates

Oral reading can occur only as fast as you can speak. The threshold for oral reading rates has been established at 140 wpm (Balogh, 2005). Oral reading at a rate of 140 wpm is a reasonable expectation for classroom assessment.

Very little data is actually available on oral reading rates of adult second-language readers. Lems (2006) has published a study showing that "oral reading fluency as a measure of adult [English language learner] silent reading becomes significant after a certain number of requisite skills are in place" (p. 246). Those requisite skills include listening comprehension, decoding, and recoding/pronunciation. This viewpoint suggests that if we are going to engage readers in fluent oral reading, helping them become strong silent readers first is important.

A threshold of silent reading rate is 250-300 wpm (Carver, 1990). As with oral fluency data, there is little actual empirical data available on the silent reading rates of second-language readers. Cushing-Weigle and Jensen (1996) report on data they gathered in university ESL classes. A primary finding from their research is that a reading rate improvement component should be included in classroom instruction.

The suggestions provided in this book give teachers input on exactly what they can do to improve both the oral and the silent reading fluency rates of students in their classes.

Reason #4: Bottom-up reading skills

Strong oral readers are able to decode words. Recall the finding from Lems (2006) that indicated that decoding was a prerequisite skill for oral reading. As has been emphasized earlier in this chapter and throughout this book, focusing on the development of strong bottom-up reading skills is essential to strong oral reading fluency. Readers should have the ability to decode each word and know how to pronounce it correctly. This process is an essential component of oral reading fluency.

Reason #5: From silent to oral reader

I cannot emphasize strongly enough the relationship between building strong silent and oral readers. If we want strong oral readers, we must have strong silent readers. Our ultimate goal as reading teachers should be the development of strong silent readers, since silent reading is the activity that our students will most frequently engage in.

Reason #6: Anxiety

Finally, many students experience anxiety in the reading classroom. Part of the anxiety comes from having to stand and read aloud. Even very confident readers can experience some degree of anxiety when asked to read aloud in front of others. I recently had this experience when asked to read in a group. I misread a word. I realized immediately that I had misread the word, but I kept moving forward in the text.

I encourage all teachers to reduce factors of anxiety and make the classroom a positive environment. I always tell my students that my classroom is the safest place in the world in which to make a mistake because then we can address the mistake so that it will not happen outside of the classroom.

Conclusions

In this section, we have focused on the important role of reading fluency; both in silent and oral reading. This is an issue that will continue to require our focused attention in the next few years as we better understand how we can blend the teaching of oral and silent reading fluency more appropriately in the reading classroom.

6. The need for more extensive reading

Think about the reading you do on a daily basis. What do you read? How long do you read? Why do you read?

Share your answers with a classmate or colleague.

Although the title "extensive reading" was not explicitly used by the reading specialists who provided their lists of priorities for reading teachers, Bamford, Grabe, and Stoller each indicated that readers need access to a lot of level-appropriate materials. Recall earlier discussions in this book about Krashen's (1982) input hypothesis ($i + 1$) and selecting appropriate reading material (pages 25–27). Teachers should help readers identify appropriate materials that fall at the $i - 1$ level. We want readers to have access to enjoyable reading material that will not be too challenging for them.

The level of vocabulary should be very familiar to the students. Readers should know approximately 95 percent of the vocabulary they encounter during extensive reading. At that level of familiarity, readers will be able to skip the five percent of the words they do not know and still have a strong level of reading comprehension.

Day and Bamford (1998) and Bamford and Day (2004) provide very good ideas for integrating extensive reading into the classroom. Both of these books provide a strong rationale for using extensive reading and over 100 suggestions from teachers all over the world who have provided activities for the classroom.

If we want our students to become better readers, there is really only one way to help them: get them to read more. Engaging them in meaningful reading does not mean that it has to be challenging and overwhelming. We want the reading to be exciting and motivating. We want them to look forward to opportunities to read.

Remember that one essential part of extensive reading is for the teacher to model the behaviors of good readers. You should share with your students what you are reading and encourage them to share with each other.

I often ask my students, whether they are ESL/EFL learners or teachers in training, what they are reading for pleasure. We cannot forget the importance of developing our own skills as readers. One of the ways that I try to do this is by reading in my second language. I have read the *Harry Potter* series in Spanish. This has provided the perfect opportunity for me to maintain my language skills and to remember what it is like to be in the shoes of the second language learner. I have enjoyed sharing with my students what I am learning about myself as a reader from reading in Spanish.

I encourage teachers (and learners) to read material in three different areas. First, I encourage you to read something every day that will help you improve as a teacher. (For learners, I encourage them to choose something to read in their intended area of study.) Second, I encourage you to read something that will help you be a better human being. Our social, emotional, and spiritual skills need to be improved and developed. Finally, I encourage you to reading something *for fun!* Do not forget the pleasures that come from reading just because you want to. We should never become so busy that we cannot read materials in these three areas every day.

Extensive reading is clearly something that should be integrated into every reading program around the world. Do not neglect this important aspect of helping your students become better readers.

Action

What are some specific things that you would do to integrate more extensive reading into a reading curriculum?

1. _____

2. _____

3. _____

4. _____

5. _____

What have you learned about extensive reading in this book that will help you in the future?

1. _____

2. _____

3. _____

4. _____

5. _____

_____

7. The need for professional development for teachers of reading

Development as a teacher is a process, not an event. Since we are all aware that simply reading this book and engaging in the activities suggested here will not be the single event that will help you as a teacher, I do hope that this book will serve as part of the process of your development as a teacher to improve the teaching of reading.

I have always felt strongly that teachers should not rely on their employers to determine their professional development needs. I think teachers should take responsibility for themselves in improving how they approach the teaching of reading.

Bailey, Curtis, and Nunan (2001) in their book *Pursuing Professional Development: The Self as Source* provide an excellent resource to guide teachers through a variety of tools that can be used for professional development and ultimately to better teaching. Self-observations, journals, videoing, action research, peer observation, team teaching, and teaching portfolios are some of the topics in the chapters of their book.

Although *Pursuing Professional Development* is not written specifically for teachers of reading, if you approach your reading of that book and implementation of the ideas within the context of a reading classroom, you will see how valuable these tools can be for improving your skills as a reading teacher.

Recall the list of priorities that you identified at the beginning of this chapter on page 131. What I would recommend that you do is develop a personal professional development plan, or what I call a "PPDP". Use the list of priorities that you identified in this chapter as a starting place. Use what you have learned from reading this book. In this way, you can continue to make improvements in your teaching.

I encourage you to share your PPDP with another teacher. Find someone whom you trust, someone who can help you see your strengths and weaknesses. This mentor or peer can review your PPDP and provide input that will help you make improvements.

Develop your personal professional development plan (PPDP). You can do that by completing the following pieces of information.

What are your most pressing needs as a teacher of reading?

_____

_____

_____

_____

Choose one of the pressing needs identified above.

_____

What tools are available to you for addressing this pressing need?

_____

_____

_____

_____

How much time do you think you need in order to adequately address this pressing need?

_____

How will you go about addressing this pressing need?

_____

_____

_____

_____

Who can you share your PPDP with?

_____

How will you know if you are making improvements in meeting this pressing need?

_____

_____

_____

_____

How could you share what you have learned with other teachers? Is there a local conference about teaching in which you could present what you have done?

_____

_____

_____

_____

After you have taken action and feel that you are making progress on the above pressing need, reassess your pressing needs, choose another one, and write another PPDP. Remember that professional development is a process, *not* an event. Also remember that you should be the one to take responsibility for your professional development.

8. Conclusion

This chapter has focused on key issues that reading teachers should keep in mind. First, we examined priorities that four reading specialists identified as important for teachers of reading. The suggestions from these specialists do not all match up, but there is no reason to believe that they should. There is so much that we need to know about teaching second-language reading that we cannot expect everyone to have 100 percent agreement on the key priorities that we should focus on.

Next, we examined five priorities that I believe are essential for teachers of reading. The areas include the role of reading strategies, the importance of bottom-up reading skills, the need for both silent and oral reading fluency, the need for more extensive reading, and the need for professional development for teachers of reading. Each area provides a rich source of research literature to help us make improvements in our teaching of reading.

As we bring this final chapter to a close, let me challenge you to *do something* with what you have read in this book. Do not now simply put the book on a shelf and forget about the ideas that have been discussed here. Look at your individual needs as a teacher. Look at the needs of the learners you work with. Develop a plan to make improvements and then share your successes and failures with others.

I hope that you feel that you are reaching your goals to improve language teaching and especially the teaching of reading from reading this book. For your own continued learning and growth, and for the learning and growth of your students, I encourage you to *do something with your knowledge.*

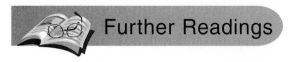
Further Readings

Bailey, K.M., A. Curtis, and D. Nunan. 2001. *Pursuing Professional Development: The self as source.* Boston, MA: Heinle & Heinle.

I would recommend that you begin your further reading with this book, which provides many ideas for how to continue your professional development as a teacher of reading.

Birch, B.M. 2007. *English L2 Reading: Getting to the bottom* (2nd ed.). Mahwah, NJ: Lawrence Erlbaum Associates.

Birch provides helpful information about the importance of building bottom-up reading strategies and integrating them with top-down strategies for a balanced, integrated approach to reading instruction.

Farstrup, A.E. and S.J. Samuels. 2002. *What Research Has to Say About Reading Instruction* (3rd ed.). Newark, DE: International Reading Association.

This excellent book provides very good articles about reading fluency instruction that are supported with research.

Helpful Websites

The International Reading Association (www.reading.org/)

Check out the resources for teachers provided by the International Reading Association at this site. You could consider joining this professional association for teachers of reading. Look for ways that you could share what you are learning in your teaching context with other members of this association.

Promoting self-regulated learning: Resources for teachers and researchers (www2.hawaii.edu/~kenton/srl/)

The student self-evaluation forms printed in Appendix 3 can be downloaded at this site.

References

Bailey, K.M., A. Curtis, and D. Nunan. 2001. *Pursuing Professional Development: The self as source.* Boston, MA: Heinle & Heinle.

Balogh, J. 2005. Measuring Adult Oral Reading. Paper presented at the Teachers of English to Speakers of Other Languages conference.

Bamford, J. and R.R. Day. (Eds.) 2004. *Extensive Reading Activities for Teaching Language.* New York, NY: Cambridge University Press.

Birch, B.M. 2007. *English L2 Reading: Getting to the bottom* (2nd ed.). Mahwah, NJ: Lawrence Erlbaum Associates.

Carver, R.P. 1990. *Reading Rate: A review of research and theory.* San Diego, CA: Academic Press.

Cushing-Weigle, S. and L. Jensen. 1996. Reading Rate Improvement in University ESL Classes. *The CATESOL Journal, 9,* 55–71.

Day, R.R. and J. Bamford. 1998. *Extensive Reading in the Second Language Classroom.* New York, NY: Cambridge University Press.

Hudson, R.F., H.B. Lane, and P.C. Pullen. 2005. Reading Fluency Assessment and Instruction: What, why, and how? *Reading Teacher, 58*(8), 702–714.

Krashen, S.D. 1982. *Principles and Practice of Second Language Acquisition.* Oxford, UK: Pergamon.

Lems, K. 2006. Reading Fluency and Comprehension in Adult English Language Learners. In T. Rasinski, C. Blachowicz, and K. Lems (Ed.) *Fluency Instruction: Research-based best practices* (pp. 231–252). New York, NY: The Guilford Press.

Panel, N.R. 2000. *Teaching Children to Read: An evidence-based assessment of the scientific research literature on reading and its implications for reading instruction.* Washington, D. C.: National Institute of Child Health and Human Development.

Samuels, S.J. 1979. The Method of Repeated Readings. *The Reading Teacher, 32,* 403–408.

Samuels, S.J. 2006. Reading Fluency: Its past, present, and future. In T. Rasinski, C. Blachowicz, and K. Lems. (Ed.) *Fluency Instruction: Research-based best practices* (pp. 7–20). New York, NY: The Guilford Press.

Snow, C.E., M.S. Burns, and P. Griffin. 1998. *Preventing Reading Difficulties in Young Children.* Washington, D.C.: National Academy Press.

Appendix 1: *Survey of Reading Strategies,* by Kouider Mokhtari and Ravi Sheorey, 2002

The purpose of this survey is to collect information about the various strategies you use when you read school-related academic materials in English (e.g., reading textbooks for homework or examinations; reading journal articles, etc.). Each statement is followed by five numbers, 1, 2, 3, 4, and 5, and each number means the following:

'1' means that 'I never or almost never do this'.
'2' means that 'I do this only occasionally'.
'3' means that 'I sometimes do this' (about 50 percent of the time).
'4' means that 'I usually do this'.
'5' means that 'I always or almost always do this'.

After reading each statement, circle the number (1, 2, 3, 4, or 5) which applies to you. Note that there are no right or wrong responses to any of the items on this survey.

Statement	Never				Always
1. I have a purpose in mind when I read.	1	2	3	4	5
2. I take notes while reading to help me understand what I read.	1	2	3	4	5
3. I think about what I know to help me understand what I read.	1	2	3	4	5
4. I take an overall view of the text to see what it is about before reading it.	1	2	3	4	5
5. When text becomes difficult, I read aloud to help me understand what I read.	1	2	3	4	5
6. I think about whether the content of the text fits my reading purpose.	1	2	3	4	5
7. I read slowly and carefully to make sure I understand what I am reading.	1	2	3	4	5
8. I review the text first by noting its characteristics like length and organization.	1	2	3	4	5
9. I try to get back on track when I lose concentration.	1	2	3	4	5
10. I underline or circle information in the text to help me remember it.	1	2	3	4	5
11. I adjust my reading speed according to what I am reading.	1	2	3	4	5
12. When reading, I decide what to read closely and what to ignore.	1	2	3	4	5
13. I use reference materials (e.g., a dictionary) to help me understand what I read.	1	2	3	4	5
14. When text becomes difficult, I pay closer attention to what I am reading.	1	2	3	4	5

15. I use tables, figures, and pictures in text to increase my understanding.   1   2   3   4   5

16. I stop from time to time and think about what I am reading.   1   2   3   4   5

17. I use context clues to help me better understand what I am reading.   1   2   3   4   5

18. I paraphrase (restate ideas in my own words) to better understand what I read.   1   2   3   4   5

19. I try to picture or visualize information to help remember what I read.   1   2   3   4   5

20. I use typographical features like bold face and italics to identify key information.   1   2   3   4   5

21. I critically analyze and evaluate the information presented in the text.   1   2   3   4   5

22. I go back and forth in the text to find relationships among ideas in it.   1   2   3   4   5

23. I check my understanding when I come across new information.   1   2   3   4   5

24. I try to guess what the content of the text is about when I read.   1   2   3   4   5

25. When text becomes difficult, I re-read it to increase my understanding.   1   2   3   4   5

26. I ask myself what questions I would like to have answered in the text.   1   2   3   4   5

27. I check to see if my guesses about the text are right or wrong.   1   2   3   4   5

28. When I read, I guess the meaning of unknown words or phrases.   1   2   3   4   5

29. When reading, I translate from English into my native language.   1   2   3   4   5

30. When reading, I think about information in both English and my mother tongue.   1   2   3   4   5

Scoring Guidelines for the *Survey of Reading Strategies*

Student Name: _____ Date: _____

1. Write the number you circled for each statement (i.e., 1, 2, 3, 4, or 5) in the appropriate blanks below.
2. Add up the scores under each column and place the result on the line under each column.
3. Divide the subscale score by the number of statements in each column to get the average for each subscale.
4. Calculate the average for the whole inventory by adding up the subscale scores and dividing by 30.
5. Use the interpretation guidelines below to understand your averages.

Global Reading Strategies (GLOB Subscale)	Problem Solving Strategies (PROB Subscale)	Support Reading Strategies (SUP Subscale)	Overall Reading Strategies (ORS)
1. _____	7. _____	2. _____	GLOB _____
3. _____	9. _____	5. _____	PROB _____
4. _____	11. _____	10. _____	SUP _____
6. _____	14. _____	13. _____	
8. _____	16. _____	18. _____	
12. _____	19. _____	22. _____	
15. _____	25. _____	26. _____	
17. _____	28. _____	29. _____	
20. _____		30. _____	
21. _____			
23. _____			
24. _____			
27. _____			

_____ GLOB Score	_____ PROB Score	_____ SUP Score	_____ Overall Score
/ 13	/ 8	/ 9	/ 30
_____ GLOB Average	_____ PROB Average	_____ SUP Average	_____ Overall Average

KEY TO AVERAGES: 3.5 or higher = High   2.5 – 3.4 = Medium   2.4 or lower = Low

INTERPRETING YOUR SCORES: The overall average indicates how often you use reading strategies when reading academic materials. The average for each subscale shows which group of strategies (i.e., global, problem solving, or support strategies) you use most often when reading. It is important to note, however, that the best possible use of these strategies depends on your reading ability in English, the type of material read, and your reading purpose. A low score on any of the subscales or parts of the inventory indicates that there may be some strategies in these parts that you might want to learn about and consider using when reading (adapted from Oxford 1990, pp. 297–300).

Mokhtari, K. and R. Sheorey. 2002. Measuring ESL Students' Awareness of Reading Strategies. *Journal of Developmental Education*, 25(3), 2–10.

Appendix 2: *Online Survey of Reading Strategies,* adapted from Kouider Mokhtari and Ravi Sheorey, 2002 by Neil J. Anderson

The purpose of this survey is to collect information about the various strategies you use when you read online in English (e.g., surfing the Internet, doing online research, etc.). Each statement is followed by five numbers, 1, 2, 3, 4, and 5, and each number means the following:

> '1' means that 'I never or almost never do this' when I read online.
> '2' means that 'I do this only occasionally' when I read online.
> '3' means that 'I sometimes do this' when I read online (about 50 percent of the time).
> '4' means that 'I usually do this' when I read online.
> '5' means that 'I always or almost always do this' when I read online.

After reading each statement, circle the number (1, 2, 3, 4, or 5) which applies to you. Note that there are no right or wrong responses to any of the items on this survey.

Statement	Never				Always
1. I have a purpose in mind when I read online.	1	2	3	4	5
2. I participate in live chat with other learners of English.	1	2	3	4	5
3. I participate in live chat with native speakers of English.	1	2	3	4	5
4. I take notes while reading online to help me understand what I read.	1	2	3	4	5
5. I think about what I know to help me understand what I read online.	1	2	3	4	5
6. I take an overall view of the online text to see what it is about before reading it.	1	2	3	4	5
7. When online text becomes difficult, I read aloud to help me understand what I read.	1	2	3	4	5
8. I think about whether the content of the online text fits my reading purpose.	1	2	3	4	5
9. I read slowly and carefully to make sure I understand what I am reading online.	1	2	3	4	5
10. I review the online text first by noting its characteristics like length and organization.	1	2	3	4	5
11. I try to get back on track when I lose concentration.	1	2	3	4	5
12. I print out a hard copy of the online text then underline or circle information to help me remember it.	1	2	3	4	5
13. I adjust my reading speed according to what I am reading online.	1	2	3	4	5
14. When reading online, I decide what to read closely and what to ignore.	1	2	3	4	5
15. I use reference materials (e.g., an online dictionary) to help me understand what I read online.	1	2	3	4	5

16. When online text becomes difficult, I pay closer attention to what I am reading.   1 2 3 4 5
17. I read pages on the Internet for academic purposes.   1 2 3 4 5
18. I use tables, figures, and pictures in the online text to increase my understanding.   1 2 3 4 5
19. I stop from time to time and think about what I am reading online.   1 2 3 4 5
20. I use context clues to help me better understand what I am reading online.   1 2 3 4 5
21. I paraphrase (restate ideas in my own words) to better understand what I read online.   1 2 3 4 5
22. I try to picture or visualize information to help remember what I read online.   1 2 3 4 5
23. I use typographical features like bold face and italics to identify key information.   1 2 3 4 5
24. I critically analyze and evaluate the information presented in the online text.   1 2 3 4 5
25. I go back and forth in the online text to find relationships among ideas in it.   1 2 3 4 5
26. I check my understanding when I come across new information.   1 2 3 4 5
27. I try to guess what the content of the online text is about when I read.   1 2 3 4 5
28. When online text becomes difficult, I re-read it to increase my understanding.   1 2 3 4 5
29. I ask myself what questions I would like to have answered in the online text.   1 2 3 4 5
30. I check to see if my guesses about the online text are right or wrong.   1 2 3 4 5
31. When I read online, I guess the meaning of unknown words or phrases.   1 2 3 4 5
32. I scan the online text to get a basic idea of whether it will serve my purposes before choosing to read it.   1 2 3 4 5
33. I read pages on the Internet for fun.   1 2 3 4 5
34. I critically evaluate the online text before choosing to use information I read online.   1 2 3 4 5
35. I can distinguish between fact and opinion in online texts.   1 2 3 4 5
36. When reading online, I look for sites that cover both sides of an issue.   1 2 3 4 5
37. When reading online, I translate from English into my native language.   1 2 3 4 5
38. When reading online, I think about information in both English and my mother tongue.   1 2 3 4 5

Scoring Guidelines for the *Online Survey of Reading Strategies*

Student Name: _____ Date: _____

1. Write the number you circled for each statement (i.e., 1, 2, 3, 4, or 5) in the appropriate blanks below.
2. Add up the scores under each column and place the result on the line under each column.
3. Divide the subscale score by the number of statements in each column to get the average for each subscale.
4. Calculate the average for the whole inventory by adding up the subscale scores and dividing by 38.
5. Use the interpretation guidelines below to understand your averages.

Global Reading Strategies (GLOB Subscale)	Problem Solving Strategies (PROB Subscale)	Support Reading Strategies (SUP Subscale)	Overall Reading Strategies (ORS)
1. _____	9. _____	4. _____	GLOB _____
2. _____	11. _____	7. _____	PROB _____
3. _____	13. _____	12. _____	SUP _____
5. _____	16. _____	15. _____	
6. _____	19. _____	21. _____	
8. _____	22. _____	25. _____	
10. _____	28. _____	29. _____	
14. _____	31. _____	37. _____	
17. _____	34. _____	38. _____	
18. _____	35. _____		
20. _____	36. _____		
23. _____			
24. _____			
26. _____			
27. _____			
30. _____			
32. _____			
33. _____			

_____ GLOB Score _____ PROB Score _____ SUP Score _____ **Overall Score**

/ 18   / 11   / 9   / 38

_____ GLOB Average _____ PROB Average _____ SUP Average _____ **Overall Average**

KEY TO AVERAGES: 3.5 or higher = High   2.5 – 3.4 = Medium   2.4 or lower = Low

INTERPRETING YOUR SCORES: The overall average indicates how often you use reading strategies when reading academic materials. The average for each subscale shows which group of strategies (i.e., global, problem solving, or support strategies) you use most often when reading. It is important to note, however, that the best possible use of these strategies depends on your reading ability in English, the type of material read, and your reading purpose. A low score on any of the subscales or parts of the inventory indicates that there may be some strategies in these parts that you might want to learn about and consider using when reading online (adapted from Oxford 1990, pp. 297–300).

Adapted from Mokhtari, K. and R. Sheorey. 2002. Measuring ESL Students Reading Strategies. *Journal of Developmental Education*, 25(3), 2–10.

Appendix 3: Managing My Own Learning, Forms A-G

Riley & Harsch, 2007, http://www2.hawaii.edu/~kenton/srl/

Worksheet A: Introduction and Discussion   *IDENTIFY/SHARE*

Name _____ Date _____

The purpose of this worksheet is to <u>identify</u> what you already know about your language learning goals, <u>describe</u> your beliefs about teacher and student roles and <u>share ideas</u> about language learning strategies (LLS) you use. Work with a partner or in small groups. Talk about and write short answers to the following questions:

1. For learning or using English, I'd like to learn how to . . .

2. To reach this goal, I believe the teacher's role and the student's role are:

Teacher's roles	Student's roles

3. Write some specific problems you have with learning or using English. (For example, I can't pronounce "R" and "L"). Then talk with classmates about possible strategies you could use to solve these problems.

Problem	Strategies to Solve or Prevent the Problem
I have a vocabulary test, and I have difficulty memorizing words.	I'm going to make some flashcards and study them on the bus.

4. Here are some examples of LLS. Read the strategies and think of problems you might have or personal situations where these strategies might be useful. Write short answers in the blanks.

Problem	Strategies to Solve or Prevent the Problem
• I have difficulty memorizing words. • I have a vocabulary test.	Writing words on Post-it ® notes and sticking them on the walls of my room, so I see them every day
• My teacher asks the class to find information about a new topic.	Using other resources (e.g., Internet, magazines, newspapers, videos)
• I want to practice pronunciation. • I want to learn new words. • I need to proofread a paper.	Reading aloud
	Paying attention to successful students' use of English
	Eavesdropping on native speakers' conversations
	Making an effort to practice speaking, listening, reading, and writing
	Finding opportunities to use English naturally
	Guessing (e.g., the meaning of words, what will happen next)
	Focusing on a skill (e.g., pronunciation, listening)
	Making positive statements about my learning
	Evaluating the difficulty of a task, activity, or project
	Making an effort to think in English
	Using my environment to learn new words
	Looking in a dictionary at other forms of a word (adj., n. v., adv.)
	Looking in a thesaurus for words with similar meaning
	Reading about the same thing in English and in my own language

CLUSTERS–clusters are strategies used in combination with others
For example: The skill of using a dictionary includes using more than one strategy, such as alphabetizing, checking spelling, using prefixes to help work out the meaning of words, selecting the correct meaning from many meanings, applying the correct meaning, and finding derivations (where words come from).
Think of some strategy "clusters" you might use connected to: a) making a telephone call b) buying a bus or train ticket c) reading a newspaper

5. Have you ever kept a list of LLS you use? (e.g., in your class textbook, in a journal or notebook, in a diary)

6. Do you ever share ideas about LLS with anyone? If yes, who with and which ideas? If no, do you think it would be useful to share ideas with others?

7. Do you ever think about any LLS you use? If no, is thinking (reflecting) about LLS useful for you? If yes, which ones were most effective for you?

8. On Worksheet B, your Personal Strategy Repertoire, write any strategies you already use. Also add new strategies from the list above or from your discussion. (If you want to, design your own "Personal Strategy Repertoire" worksheet.)

Managing My Own Learning

Riley & Harsch, 2007, http://www2.hawaii.edu/~kenton/srl/

Worksheet B: Personal Strategy Repertoire *CONNECT*

Name _____ Date _____

As you discover and use new strategies, add them to your repertoire.

In the column headed *S/D*, write an *S* if the use of the strategy was successful or a *D* if it was difficult. In the column headed *R/A*, write an *R* if you used the strategy to react to a learning challenge or an *A* if you used the strategy to anticipate a learning challenge.

Write *C* next to the strategy if you used it as part of a "cluster" (combined with other strategies).

Strategy	I use this when...	S/D	R/A

Managing My Own Learning

Riley & Harsch, 2007, http://www2.hawaii.edu/~kenton/srl/

Worksheet C: Ongoing Language Experiences *REFLECT*

Name _____ Date _____

Write about your experience learning or using English this week (either in class or outside). Describe the situations and the strategies you used. You can choose to write about one or more of these:

- A <u>successful experience</u> learning or using English that you had this week
  What strategies or clusters of strategies did you use that helped you succeed?

- A <u>difficult experience</u> learning or using English that you had this week
  What strategies or clusters of strategies could you use to improve in this area?

- <u>Strategies your classmates shared</u> about learning or using English

Language Situations or Problems	Strategies to Solve or Prevent the Problem

Put * next to the strategies that you feel are very useful.

Draw lines connecting strategies you combined.

About what percentage of time did you use English outside the classroom? _____%

❏ Do you want feedback from the teacher about what you have written? (check the box)
  Do you have a question for your teacher? Write it here:

_____

_____

Checkpoint: "I am responsible for my own learning". To what extent is this true of me this week?

1	2	3	4	5
never true	hardly ever true	sometimes true	often true	always true

Managing My Own Learning

Riley & Harsch, 2007, http://www2.hawaii.edu/~kenton/srl/

Worksheet D: Language Experiences Summary *REFLECT*

Name _____ Date _____

The purpose of this worksheet is to look back over all your Worksheet C and Personal Strategy Repertoire to give a picture of the range of language learning strategies (LLS) you use and how you manage your own learning.

1. How many Worksheet Cs did you complete? _____. Do you think this is enough?_____

2. Think about which LLS worked for your learning purposes.

3. Of these, choose the Top Five LLS.

4. Write them in the table below.

5. Explain *why* you thought they worked for you.

6. Look again at your Top Five strategies. Did you:
   a) react to a problem and try to find a solution? (R)
   b) anticipate a problem and try to prevent it? (A)

LLS I used that worked	Why my Top Five LLS worked	R = React A = Anticipate

7. For any that you checked *React*, did you learn anything that could change it to *Anticipate*?

_____

_____

_____

8. Add any Top Five items to your Personal Strategy Repertoire that are not already there.

9. Take time to think about everything you have experienced by writing these reflection forms. Do you have a <u>specific</u> personal goal or goals for your future language learning? If so, write it here.

_____

_____

_____

10. In what way have your goals changed since you began managing your own learning?

_____

_____

_____

11. Look over all your Checkpoints on Worksheet C and fill in the chart.

Checkpoint: "I am responsible for my own learning." To what extent is this true of me this week?												
5 = always true												
4 = often true												
3 = sometimes true												
2 = hardly ever true												
1 = never true												
week	1	2	3	4	5	6	7	8	9	10	11	12
Checkpoint: % of English I used outside class – (copy from your Worksheet Cs)												

12. Can you describe a pattern?

_____

_____

_____

13. How does this process help you become better at managing your own learning?

_____

_____

_____

Managing My Own Learning

Riley & Harsch, 2007, http://www2.hawaii.edu/~kenton/srl/

Worksheet E: Peer Interview   *SHARE & CONNECT*

Name _____ Date _____

Look over Worksheets B, C, and D to help answer the questions.

Choose a classmate to interview. Ask questions and write answers in the chart.

My classmate's name	My classmate's answers
What strategy or strategies worked for you? Why?	
What strategy or strategies didn't work? Why not?	
Which strategies did you use in clusters? (combined)	
Did you try to use any strategies from other sources? (from classmates, textbooks, other materials such as TV, video).	
Did you try out any of the teacher's feedback? If so, what?	
What are your specific goals for language learning?	

Look over your interview notes. What important things do you notice about the information from your classmates? Write two sentences in the box. Samples: *a) Saori recommended watching DVDs with and without sub-titles. b) Masanori mostly tried to guess meanings of words when reading.*

Compare yourself with your classmate. Write your answer in the box.

1.	What LLS did your classmate use that you didn't?
2.	Would you add them to your repertoire? Why? Why not?

Update your Personal Repertoire.

Managing My Own Learning

Riley & Harsch, 2007, http://www2.hawaii.edu/~kenton/srl/

Worksheet F: Oral Presentation   *SHARE & CONNECT*

Name _____   Date _____

Look over all of your Worksheets B, C, D, and E. Think about your learning experiences.

Here are some statements to help you think about this:

1.	I wrote _____ Worksheets Cs. (How many?)
2.	The strategies that worked best for me were:
3.	I liked these strategies because:
4.	The strategies that didn't work were:
5.	A strategy I recommend trying is:
6.	A cluster of strategies I recommend trying are:
7.	I also tried to use strategies in our textbook or class materials. These were:
8.	The most important thing I learned about managing my own learning was:
9.	My goal to help me be a better language learner in the future is:

Outline of My Presentation:

Oral Presentation – *speaking about my language learning experiences*

1. Use your outline notes and talk about something that you think is interesting, important, or useful about your language learning experiences that you want to share with your classmates.

2. Listen to your classmates' ideas. Write any new LLS you like in the box.

New LLS I learned from my classmates

Update your Personal Strategy Repertoire.

Managing My Own Learning

Riley & Harsch, 2007, http://www2.hawaii.edu/~kenton/srl/

Worksheet G: Newsletter   *SHARE & CONNECT*

Name _____ Date _____

The purpose of this task is to share language learning strategies (LLSs) and discover what others have used.

1. Form groups of three to four.

2. Share your Top Five LLS from Worksheet D, and together agree on your group's Top 10.

3. Choose one group member to:
a) type the list into a Word file and send it to your teacher, or
b) write the list on the form below and hand it to your teacher.

4. Your teacher will combine each group's Top 10 into a class newsletter and give a copy to everyone.

5. When you have this copy, look over all the strategies. Which ones could be clusters?

Top 10 LLS	Why they worked

Glossary

acceptable word method – a method of scoring cloze tests in which any grammatical answer that makes sense in context is accepted as correct. Contrasted with the **exact word method**

achievement test – a test used at the end of a unit or a course to see if readers learned the reading skills that were taught in the class

approach – a general, philosophical orientation to language teaching

automaticity theory – being highly skilled at certain tasks and able to devote attention to doing more than one thing

bottom-up processing – a focus on the smallest units of meaning (e.g., sounds, letters, letter combinations, words)

content area – a school subject area such as history, science, philosophy, etc.

content word – a word that expresses substantive meaning, including nouns, verbs, adverbs, and adjectives. Contrasted with **function word**

corpus – a large collection of written or spoken texts

diagnostic test – a test administered usually at the beginning of a class to provide detailed input to a teacher on what students already know how to do and what they still need to learn

digraph – two consonant letters that make one sound (e.g., *sh, ch, th, ck, ph*)

diphthong – a vowel that sounds like a combination of two vowels (e.g., the vowel sound in *tail*)

English as a Foreign Language (EFL) – the study of English in an environment where English is not the language of communication outside of the classroom (e.g., learning English in Brazil or Korea)

English as a Second Language (ESL) – the study of English in an environment where English is the language of communication outside of the classroom (e.g., learning English in Canada or New Zealand)

exact word method – a method of scoring cloze tests in which only the original words from the complete text are accepted as correct answers. Contrasted with the **acceptable word method**

extensive reading – reading increased amounts of a variety of texts

false beginner – a student who has studied English but has not had an opportunity to speak it extensively and thus lacks fluency, confidence, breadth of vocabulary, or easy mental access to grammar rules to apply when speaking

fluent reading – reading at an appropriate rate (200 words per minute) with adequate comprehension (70 percent)

function word – a word that serves a grammatical function but do not express substantive meaning, including articles (e.g., *a, an, the*) and prepositions (e.g., *above, up, down*) Contrasted with **content word**

graphic organizer – a visual representation to show relationships among ideas in a text

headword – the most important word in a word family

input hypothesis – a language learning hypothesis proposed by Professor Stephen Krashen. The hypothesis is stated as $i + 1$. The hypothesis states that input (language which a learner learns or receives) needs to be just above the current level of the learner.

intensive reading – reading a short text with the goal of practicing a specific reading strategy

interactive approach to reading – a combination of both bottom-up and top-down approaches to reading

intermediate level slump – the transition from learning to reading to reading to learn, characterized by a slowing of progress due to students' belief that they are more advanced than they really are

L2 – second language, the language being taught in an ESL or EFL context

lexical strategy – a strategy that focuses on learning words of a language

metacognitive strategy – a strategy for reflecting on your own thinking

morpheme – a unit of meaning that is either "free" (a word that can stand alone) or "bound (a grammatical marker such as –*ing* or –*ed* that, in order to have meaning, must be attached to a word)

orthographic strategy – a strategy that focuses on learning the writing system of a language

phonics approach – learning the sounds for individual letters

phonological strategy – a strategy that focuses on pronouncing words correctly

placement test – a test used to place students, often by level of reading ability, into a class with students of the same abilities

process approach to writing – an approach that breaks teaching writing into smaller parts that are easy for students to learn

progress test – a test that provides specific information on the improvements readers are making and what reading skills are being mastered as they read

qualitative assessment – an assessment that focuses on quality and is typically not measurable through numbers

quantitative assessment – an assessment that is measurable through numbers

reading fluency – reading at an adequate rate (approximately 200 words per minute) with adequate comprehension (70%)

reading skill – an unconscious action that readers take while reading. A reading skill is a strategy that has become automatic in its use.

reading strategy – a conscious action that readers take to improve their reading

special vowel sound – a term sometimes used for **diphthong** in the teaching of phonics.

strategic reading – the ability of the reader to use a wide variety of reading strategies to accomplish a purpose for reading

syllabus – part of a curriculum that outlines the content to be taught in a textbook or a program of study

syntactic strategy – a strategy that is focused on syntax or grammar of a language

top-down processing – using larger contexts (e.g., background knowledge) to process meaning

whole language approach – a theory of teaching that emphasizes comprehension and fluency over skill instruction

word family – a group of words that share a similar base (e.g., *happy, happily,* and *happiness*)

word web – a visual representation of relationships among various words

Index

Credits

p. 33 From *Reading Advantage 1 2nd edition* by Casey Malarcher, 2004. Reprinted with permission of Heinle/ELT, a division of Thomson Learning: www.thomsonrights.com. **p. 34** From *Strategic Reading Level 1* by Jack C. Richards and Samuela Eckstut-Didier, 2003. Reprinted with the permission of Cambridge University Press. **p. 35** From *Read and Reflect 1* by Jayme Adelson-Goldstein and Lori Howard, 2004, Oxford University Press. **p. 37** From *NorthStar Focus on Reading and Writing: Basic/Low Intermediate* by Beth Maher and Natasha Haugnes, 2003. **p. 39** From *ACTIVE Skills for Reading - Intro. 1st edition* by Neil Anderson, 2008. Reprinted with permission of Heinle/ELT, a division of Thomson Learning: www.thomsonrights.com. **p. 41** From *ACTIVE Skills for Reading, Book 1 2nd edition* by Neil Anderson, 2007. Reprinted with permission of Heinle/ELT, a division of Thomson Learning: www.thomsonrights.com. **p. 42** From *ACTIVE Skills for Reading, Book 1, 2nd edition* by Neil Anderson, 2007. Reprinted with permission of Heinle/ELT, a division of Thomson Learning: www.thomsonrights.com. **p. 44** From *ACTIVE Skills for Reading, Book 1, 2nd edition* by Neil Anderson, 2007. Reprinted with permission of Heinle/ELT, a division of Thomson Learning: www.thomsonrights.com. **p. 74** From *NorthStar Intermediate, Reading and Writing 2e* by Carolyn Dupaquier-Sardinas and Laurie Barto, 2004. **p. 77** From *ACTIVE Skills for Reading - Intro. 1st edition* by Neil Anderson, 2008. Reprinted with permission of Heinle/ELT, a division of Thomson Learning: www.thomsonrights.com. **p. 80** From *Extensive Reading Activities for Teaching Language* by Julian Bamford and Richard R. Day, 2004. Reprinted with the permission of Cambridge University Press. **pp. 105-107** From *Essential Academic Vocabulary, Mastering the Complete Academic Word List 1st edition* by Huntley, 2006. Reprinted with permission of Heinle/ELT, a division of Thomson Learning: www.thomsonrights.com. **pp. 109-110** From *Focus on Vocabulary* by Diane Schmitt and Norbert Schmitt. **pp. 115-116** From *More Reading Power* by Beatrice S. Mikulecky and Linda Jeffries, 2002. **p. 120** Screen shot of Lexxica homepage, www.lexxica.com. **pp. 120** "Self-regulated learning forms" by Lesley Riley and Kenton Harsch from www2.hawaii.edu. Reprinted by permission of Kenton Harsch. **Reflection Icon:** EyeWire/Getty Images. **Action Icon:** David Buffington/Getty Images.

We apologize for any apparent infringement of copyright and if notified, the publisher will be pleased to rectify any errors or omissions at the earliest opportunity.